A
BALKAN
MISSION

THE MEETING OF EAST AND WEST
SARAJEVO FROM THE MOHAMMEDAN QUARTER

A
BALKAN
MISSION

By JAMES T. SHOTWELL

Published in New York 1949 by
COLUMBIA UNIVERSITY PRESS

*Published in Great Britain, Canada, and India by
Geoffrey Cumberlege, Oxford University Press,
London, Toronto, and Bombay*

MANUFACTURED IN THE UNITED STATES OF AMERICA

TO MY FELLOW TRAVELER
IN THIS AND A MUCH LONGER
JOURNEY

Prefatory Note

THIS story of a journey through the Balkan countries is chiefly drawn from letters written at the time and from notes jotted down from day to day in the course of travel. To this text, which is largely reproduced in its original form there have been added notes and comments both to explain events and personalities then familiar but now partly forgotten and to make clear the setting of this episode in the light of subsequent history.

J. T. S.

New York
October 14, 1948

Contents

Illustrations

1 · A Balkan Assignment

Although this story is mostly the personal narrative of a journey through the Balkans in the autumn of 1925, it is also the record of an assignment by the Carnegie Endowment for International Peace which had a dual purpose.

In the first place, I was to make arrangements in each of the five countries, Yugoslavia, Rumania, Bulgaria, Turkey, and Greece, for the completion of the *Economic and Social History of the World War*, a task upon which I had been engaged for the previous five years. This had grown out of a plan which I had submitted to the Endowment as early as the autumn of 1914 for the study of the data of modern war and its impact upon a world at peace. The plan was held in abeyance throughout the war years, but immediately after the close of the Paris Peace Conference, in which I was a member of the American Delegation, the plan was revived with little change and I was asked to undertake its direction.

So many books have now been written on the nature of war that it is difficult even to imagine the lack of them in the literature of that time. Although there had been studies on the technical aspects of war and some penetrating analyses of war economics, there were no models to which one could refer as guides in a comprehensive effort to measure the disturbances created by war in the processes of modern life. This was largely because, from the days of Herodotus down, war had been accepted as a military fact of political history, and its economic and social effects had lain outside the scope of either history or economics. Historians of war had concentrated upon its drama, and most economists had ignored its cost or had been satisfied with traditional expression of opinion. The World War had offered an unparalleled laboratory of experience and the Carnegie Endowment an unrivaled opportunity for drawing the lessons which it presented.

Recognizing that no single study would ever be adequate to deal with so large a subject as the impact of the World War upon the conditions of life in the countries of Europe, the War History had been planned as a vast enterprise with organized boards of editors in each country who could enlist the interest and secure the cooperation of those best qualified, either by high office in wartime or by special technical competence, to leave a permanent record of the way in which this First World War had changed the conditions and the lives of so many people. By 1925 over thirty wartime cabinet ministers and some two hundred of their associates of varying rank had been engaged upon the preparation of these volumes, the scope of which included even the history of wartime Russia. But as yet only very tentative and unsatisfactory plans had been undertaken to cover the war history of the part of Europe in which the war itself began. The experience in other countries had shown that this could not be done satisfactorily without personal contact with editors and authors. We had to enlist the interest and secure the cooperation, not only of students of public affairs, but of wartime administrators who knew through experience what had actually taken place during and after the war. To keep a unity of plan and purpose in such a vast and intricate field was the task of the Director of the History. It was one which could not be performed at long range, but involved personal contacts and discussions with collaborators.

Neither from Paris, the Continental headquarters of the Endowment, nor from Vienna, where I maintained a regular editorial staff, was it possible to plan for the volumes dealing with Southeastern Europe. Not only was it necessary for the editor to gain a personal impression, if only an inadequate one, of the postwar situation of those countries, but it was equally important for the Endowment as the sponsor of the History to show that its interest was not confined to the powers of Western Europe. Therefore, it was decided to settle the plans for the volumes dealing with the Balkan countries in conferences in Belgrade, Bucharest, Sofia, Constantinople, and Athens.

In addition to this work on the War History, there was also another reason for the Endowment to entrust me with a mission to the Balkans. It was there that the Endowment had undertaken its first major task, an investigation of the atrocities committed in the Second Balkan War. The report of its Commission, published in 1913, while forgotten history in other parts of the world, had by no means been forgotten in the Balkans, where throughout centuries of Turkish rule these mountain peoples cherished the memory of ancient wrongs. An international investigation of atrocities on the spot where they had occurred was something very different from the protests against the cruelties of the Turk, even when voiced by a Gladstone or chronicled in *The Times*. The plan of the Endowment, which was due to its European Chairman, Baron d'Estournelles de Constant, personal friend of Mr. Carnegie and one of the leaders of enlightened opinion in Western Europe, was to send to the Macedonian battlefields a commission of distinguished jurists and authorities on international affairs, counting upon the impact of its report upon public opinion to further the cause of peace in Europe. It was a bold innovation in European politics for an unofficial body of this kind to undertake an investigation on the conduct of war by an inquiry which involved the consent and, to some extent, the cooperation of the governments concerned. Fortunately for the Endowment the Bulgars, profiting from the advice of Arthur Bullard, an American correspondent who had accompanied their armies, accepted the Endowment plan of investigation and the Serbian and Greek governments followed their example, although allowing somewhat less freedom of investigation to the Commission.

The result was that when the report of the Commission appeared, the Serbians felt that their case had not been fully stated and charged that its conclusions had been unfair to them. The initial resentment which this had caused had been largely overcome by American aid to Serbia during and after the War and especially by the magnificent gift of a Carnegie Library to the University of Belgrade.

The World War followed too quickly upon the Balkan Wars for this first major effort of the Endowment to achieve its effect upon the public opinion of Europe, which now was shocked by atrocities of war committed on so much greater a scale that the sufferings of the victims which this report so graphically described seemed almost minor incidents in the history of violence.

Parallel with this description of the conduct of war, the Endowment undertook a study of the political situation which had been created by the overthrow of the Turkish Empire. Both in history and in politics, the Balkan countries had always been viewed in the West as part of the Near Eastern Question, and properly so because down to 1912, when they formed the Balkan Coalition against the Turks, it was the great powers which arranged the sad and sordid game of diplomacy in which the Balkan people were the pawns and generally the victims. The wars of liberation, however, far from bringing peace, had acted as a spur to nationalism, the hot center of which was the unsettled frontier of Macedonia.

To throw light upon this situation the Endowment secured the services of George W. Young, one of the most competent of British diplomats, who, from his posts in Constantinople and in the Balkan countries, had been a close student of the rise of Balkan nationalism and its interplay with European politics, while at the same time, as was shown by his great codification of Ottoman law, *Corps de Droit Ottoman,* he was thoroughly familiar with the Turkish background of these questions. His volume, *Nationalism and War in the Near East,* published anonymously because of the author's former official position in the British foreign service, was completed in August, 1914, in the opening weeks of the World War, and in spite of its richness of detail and mastery of style, it passed almost unnoticed while the vastly greater drama of the World War held the attention of all. The opportunity had now come to follow up this study of *Nationalism and War in the Near East* by adding the Balkan countries and Turkey to those already within the Endowment's *Economic and Social History of the World War.*

While this was the main justification for my journey to the Balkans, there was also other work to be done in the more practical field of international relations. The terms of reference for this part of my program of work were stated in a letter from President Nicholas Murray Butler:

(1) To explain to them in such detail as may seem advisable the organization, plan of work, and ideals of the Carnegie Endowment;

(2) to learn from them what may be the more interesting and more pressing problems bearing upon international cooperation and international understanding; and

(3) to get their suggestions as to forms or kinds of work which the Endowment might undertake that would in their opinion be of benefit in their part of the world as an aid to the accomplishment of the Endowment's purposes.

The Balkan assignment fitted in perfectly with the rest of my work for the Endowment. From the Paris Peace Conference on, I had been living most of the time in Europe and had seen at first hand and in close contact much of the political and economic life of those postwar years. It was, therefore, inevitable that my studies in the history of the War should lead to a growing preoccupation with the problems of war prevention, most of which, but not all, centered in Geneva. In the autumn of 1923, while on a visit to New York, I had formed a committee designed to study in detail the problems then before the League,* and in the spring

*The members of this committee were General Tasker H. Bliss, formerly of the Supreme War Council; Dr. Isaiah Bowman, Chief of the technical experts of the American Delegation at the Paris Peace Conference; Professor Joseph Chamberlain, Columbia University; Professor John Bates Clark, Director of the Division of Economics and History of the Carnegie Endowment for International Peace; Dr. Stephen P. Duggan, Director of the Institute of International Education; General James G. Harbord, former Chief of Staff of the American Army; Dr. F. P. Keppel, President of the Carnegie Corporation; David Hunter Miller, legal adviser to President Wilson at the Paris Peace Conference; Dr. Henry S. Pritchett, President of the Carnegie Foundation, and Dr. James T. Shotwell.

of 1924 we had drafted "A Practical Plan for Disarmament," which went still farther than Lord Cecil's committee of the League toward the creation of the Protocol of Geneva of 1924, which in the opinion of the historians of the League marks the height of its achievement in the clarification of the joint problem of security and disarmament. The fact that this protocol had been finally rejected by the new Conservative government of Great Britain, after it had been accepted, in theory at least, by the Continental powers led ultimately to the substitute plans of the Treaty of Locarno of August, 1925. This meant that a new center for educational work in this field was opening up in Germany itself and, leaving the visit to the Balkans for the autumn, I spent the summer principally in Geneva and Germany, working with my German colleagues on the problems of disarmament and security which were still on the agenda of the League of Nations, to which it was confidently expected that Germany would be admitted—a hope that took definite shape in the negotiations at Locarno.

This is not the place to develop further the story of the combinations which lay behind the planning of the League of Nations to deal with its most serious peacetime problem, but there is every reason to emphasize the importance of Geneva at that time as the political center of Europe. It is not too much to say that the first chapter of any journey of the kind which we were to undertake, especially to Southeastern Europe, began best at Geneva. No matter what the individual preferences of the traveler might be, he would learn in Geneva how best to arrange the program of his journey and would find later, upon arrival at the capitals of the different countries, the advantage of beginning in the neutral atmosphere of the city of the League of Nations.

This fact was accepted more or less as an axiom by the governments of the different Balkan countries even when they had a grievance against the activities of the League. In the first place, Geneva was the conciliation center where the chief problem of international disagreement in Eastern and Southern Europe was dealt with—that of minorities. Questions like this forced even those statesmen who otherwise would have little interest in the activities of the League to follow closely everything proposed in Council or Assembly. Everywhere in political circles in the Near East the influence of the League could be appreciated if one looked closely at the trend of policy, although at times it seemed a rather subconscious influence like that exerted by the press upon public men through fear of publicity. The potential influence of the League over critical incidents was naturally direct and forcible enough, as the Greek-Bulgar incident of 1925 was to show —an incident which should stand out more definitely than is possible in the narrative which follows. But during the normal peaceful relations of the different states, the chief interest in Geneva of the countries of this part of Europe was in the question of minorities.

It was not, however, because questions like these are centered at Geneva that I began the journey there, for if the survey were to be of any value to the Endowment, one had to avoid becoming involved in just this sort of controversial question. The influence of an unofficial American institution in that part of the world can be ruined overnight if it were to seem to take sides with one government or another in the charges or countercharges that refer to the treatment of their nationals by their neighbors. Consequently, through the entire journey, the minority question was distinctly and definitely ignored, although at first thought one might imagine this to be one of the chief reasons for a mission from an endowment engaged in a work of conciliation.

There was a still stronger reason, however, for starting the Balkan journey at Geneva. When the Assembly met there, it became a sort of Balkan capital where one might meet in a single day with practically all of the foreign ministers of the different states and other members of their governments, as well as influential delegations drawn from their intellectual leaders. In the two Assembly meetings which I attended at Geneva I met no less than ten cabinet ministers from the countries of Southeastern Europe which I was to visit.

If Geneva was an important center for Balkan politics, it was still more important for the Balkan politicians. In the League of Nations they had their one opportunity to play a part on the larger arena of European politics as a whole; and this fact was not without its importance in estimating the prestige which the League enjoyed among the statesmen who attended it or who were candidates to the annual delegations of the Assembly. M. Duca, the Foreign Minister of Rumania, was in 1925 the Chairman of the Commission which dealt with the problem of disarmament and security. M. Politis, the distinguished Greek jurist and states-man, whose name might otherwise have remained almost un-known except among the Greeks themselves and students of inter-national law, on one historic occasion seized the opportunity to reply to the Prime Minister of Great Britain in a statement on the problem of security as seen by the smaller nations and won for himself an international reputation such as is generally reserved for statesmen of the great powers. Without the League of Na-tions, M. Beneš could hardly have established himself as an out-standing influence among all the nations. In 1925, it was the Foreign Minister of Yugoslavia, M. Nintchitch, who was Presi-dent of the Assembly. The fact that Germany was admitted to the League under his presidency was commented upon universally in all the Balkan papers. The delegation of Bulgaria, as a smaller state and a former ally of the Central Powers, had received no such distinctions yet as those of its neighbors, but the fact that Bulgaria was a ward of the League of Nations made its govern-ment follow with even closer interest every activity of the League which might affect Bulgarian questions, and at Geneva the Bul-garian Delegates were happy to meet on equal terms with their colleagues of the late enemy states.

With reference to the planning of the Balkan trip itself, I had already, before leaving for Europe, received a cabled invitation from M. Duca to meet with him in Geneva and to plan things to-gether. We had become acquainted the previous year in connec-tion with the debates on the Protocol. With the cable came a formal invitation to be the guest of the Rumanian Government during my visit to Rumania.

News of this kind travels swiftly around in foreign offices. I was not surprised, therefore, when in Geneva the Prime Minister of Bulgaria, M. Tsankoff, and the Foreign Minister, M. Kalfoff, also extended to me, without any gesture on my part, a very cordial invitation to go to Bulgaria as the guest of the Bulgarian Government.

Plans for the visit to Yugoslavia were somewhat different. I had accepted the invitation of the University of Belgrade to give two lectures there under the auspices of the American Yugoslav Society, an organization whose President was General Bliss and of whose Executive Committee I had also been a member. The Yugoslav Society also made arrangements to have as my companion on the journey through that country Bishop Nicolai Velimirovitch, distinguished ecclesiastic, who had the unique distinction of an Oxford degree and who had preached effectively in English during his years of wartime exile in England. In view of these arrangements, Minister Nintchitch and the Yugoslav delegation in Geneva asked me to accept the hospitality of their government insofar as my other plans permitted and, in any case, to regard my visit to Yugoslavia as having their cordial support.

It was not long before I also received a very pressing invitation from Poland through their Foreign Minister, Count Skrzynski, but as Poland was not on the direct line of my journey, I was obliged to decline.

Plans for the visit to Greece and Turkey could not well be made in Geneva because they would have to depend too much upon the uncertainties of two months' travel in the northern countries. Moreover, I was not particularly anxious to visit Greece under the auspices of the government then in power, that of M. Pangalos, a reactionary and corrupt government. Diplomacy, however, continued to work and later on, when I reached Bucharest, I received an official invitation from the Greek Government, which of course it was necessary to accept. My visit to Turkey, however, was entirely devoid of any attention from the government.

The decision not to investigate international questions like those of minorities, or any other outstanding difficulties in the field of practical politics, naturally closed to me avenues of information concerning topics of the greatest interest. But on the other hand, the degree of cordiality with which I was welcomed in each country may, to some extent, have depended upon this self-denying ordinance. As a matter of fact, whatever irritations may have still existed in the international relations of these countries, they recognized that settlement of these problems was now in the hands of the League of Nations, and that it was no part of the Carnegie Endowment even to seem to evince an interest in negotiations already working toward agreements. Indeed, such interference would almost certainly injure the prospects of the settlement itself and make still more difficult the work of the responsible authorities.

It was not difficult to avoid these matters and to give a quasi-academic appearance to the journey to the Balkans by keeping to the fore the planning of the volumes on the History of the War and by accepting invitations to address learned academies and universities. Most of these public occasions were attended by members of the government, and contacts were maintained with foreign offices at almost every stage of the journey. But the topics which were discussed in these personal meetings and those which were treated in the public addresses dealt with general lines of policy and carefully avoided questions of current politics. No hint was ever given as to the justice of this or that arrangement of boundaries or the treatment of populations, although there were many attempts to bring those subjects up. At the same time, practical suggestions were not lacking as to the direction of Balkan policy as a whole and in the furtherance of conciliatory measures.

In spite of the cordial reception accorded to these efforts, both public and private, to enlist the interest of influential people in the aims and purposes of the Endowment, it would have been naive in the extreme if we had expected any serious lasting results from so short a visit to people still confused by the effects of the World War and by the new political situation caused by the fall of the Hapsburg and Romanov monarchies. The confusion was not lessened by the fact that the United States had abstained from participation in Geneva in the very policies which the European statesmen regarded as essential for the maintenance of a lasting peace. As will be apparent later, I attempted in my report to the Carnegie Endowment to ensure some permanence to the efforts of its emissary by calling upon it to support continuing bodies which could carry on adult education on problems involving international relationships and the technique of the peaceful settlement of disputes. None of this, however, came to fruition, and the one lasting influence of the visit to the Balkans turned out to be the volumes which we planned together on the Economic and Social History of the World War. The invitation to join the company of scholars and statesmen who had been chosen in other countries meant much to the intellectual leaders of the Balkan countries. It was definitely a matter of pride in each of the Balkan capitals that their country would be represented in the great War History, a pride which was justified later by the high quality of their scientific work.

It was in connection with the War History, however, that an episode occurred which delayed my journey to the Balkans. This was a meeting with my Italian and Austrian colleagues which took place at Fasano on Lake Garda the week before I left Venice for the Balkans.

It had been my hope in the early days of the making of the War History that later on the chief contributors and editors of the different countries could be brought together in an international conference to compare their points of view and draw general conclusions from the work as a whole. This, as I phrased it in a proposal at the time, could have been the nucleus for an international academy on world peace. Unfortunately it was not possible to carry out this plan because the work was finished at different times in different countries and one had to face the disappointing fact as well that the interest in the economic consequences of the war lessened steadily with the passing of time, yielding to the more compelling interests of the present and future. The failure of the original plan has always been a matter of deep regret for, while it might not have provided any single set of principles equally acceptable to all countries, it would have challenged public opinion in a way that was sadly needed in the years that followed.

In the absence of a general European conference of this kind it proved possible, however, to arrange this meeting at Fasano of the Italian editorial board with Professor Wieser, the chief Editor of the Austro-Hungarian series and one of the most distinguished economists of Europe. The Chairman of the Italian board, Professor Luigi Einaudi, already recognized as the leading economist of Italy, had even then drawn from the study of the economy of Italy in the First World War the principles which guided him after the Second World War to save that economy from the catastrophe of inflation which seemed inevitable and thus to save not only Italy but all Western Europe, a service for which his election in 1948 to be first President of the Italian Republic was not too great a reward.

Professor Einaudi and his colleagues, while recognizing Professor Wieser's position as the last great exponent of the Austrian school of economists, had been more influenced by the English thinkers, especially Marshall. I could not help recalling as I listened to the debate on the fundamental principles of war economics that Professor Einaudi's library in Turin contained a larger collection of the writings of English economists than I had ever seen in any other Continental library, public or private. The interplay between the Austrian school of economists and those of Oxford and Cambridge was equally direct, although Wieser's political philosophy, as set forth in his great work, "The Law of Power" [*Das Gesetz der Macht*], reflects the Austrian world in which he lived in its endeavor to reconcile bureaucratic control with freedom, a concept utterly foreign to English thought.

It was an unforgettable experience to discuss these high themes in that villa by Lake Garda hour by hour, so absorbed in the debate as to forget for the time being the incredible beauty of the gemlike lake stretching out from the foot of the hills between the dark Italian cypress groves. No record was kept of a conversation which was carried on in English, German, and Italian, but it was agreed that the Protocol of Geneva of 1924 and the more recent treaties of Locarno had embodied the fundamental lessons from the economics of war which had been the chief concern of our study throughout the postwar years. The mass of evidence which had been accumulated but strengthened the principle upon which the Protocol was based and to which Locarno gave partial application, namely, that the revolution which had taken place in the conduct of war had involved at the same time a revolution in the conduct of international politics. For war could no longer be regarded as that instrument of national policy which was "the last argument of states," because total war could no longer be controlled by a state system based upon the old international law which sought to lessen but not to eliminate the right of warfare. The world had definitely shown that with the inevitable increase in scientific capacity for destruction mankind had come to a turning point in history which made a resort to war for the purpose of national aggrandizement not only illegal but criminal. These principles which had been set forth in Geneva were substantiated to the full by the conclusions inherent in the *Economic and Social History of the World War*.

This theme, so solidly established, became the subject of most of my talks in the Balkans, although in order to be understood the statement of it had to be adjusted to circumstances which at first sight seemed strangely at variance with it. For it must be remembered that the Balkan peoples had only recently won their freedom by resort to war and that at least two of them, the Serbs and Rumanians, had apparently profited greatly from the World War, while the Turks had used it successfully against the Greeks.

But this is anticipating. And we must now turn to the story of the Balkan journey.

The journey was a very exhausting one, lasting somewhat over two months. The itinerary through Yugoslavia began on the Dalmatian coast, then by automobile to Montenegro, through Bosnia and Serbia to Belgrade. Relatively short trips were made to Neustadt in Slovenia and to Zagreb in Croatia. Then we traveled by train and automobile through old Serbia and southwest Macedonia to the frontiers of Greece and Albania. From Serbia we went down the Danube to Rumania where, centering at Bucharest, we traveled many hundreds of miles through Transylvania towns and countryside.

By this time the season had advanced so far that motor trips through Bulgaria were abandoned, as well as the plan to visit Asia Minor from Constantinople. In Greece conditions were unfavorable for a lengthy survey, and we remained almost entirely in Athens. It might be mentioned that, in order to save time, some sixteen nights were spent traveling by train or boat—a none too happy experience in that part of the world.

In the course of the journey I delivered thirteen public addresses, not including those at banquets and luncheons. Six of these were delivered in French, the rest in English with translations in the native tongues wherever that was necessary. With one or two exceptions, there were no written texts of these addresses for they had to be adjusted to situations which only became clear at the time of their delivery. Therefore, there is little record of them except that of the summaries in the daily press or in one or two instances a stenographic report more or less garbled. Nevertheless, some of these items are given in the Appendix.

The narrative which follows is drawn from penciled notes along the journey and letters written at the time. In the years which have intervened, the memories of incidents along the way have naturally become less and less distinct, and yet the impression of most of what we saw and heard remains stronger than that of any other experience in many years of travel in Western

Europe. For the Balkans have a charm, both in landscape and in the people themselves, which is distinctive and lasting. Moving now out of the Middle Ages, in which they have remained until our day, they face a world of difficulty and uncertainty with an outlook that, if properly guided, promises hope for the future.

2 · The Dalmatian Coast

DOWN TO OUR DAY there were two gateways to the Balkans: one was the overland route from Vienna to Constantinople, the other the sea route down the Adriatic to the Aegean and beyond. In recent history it has been the land route which has received all attention. For, with the decline of the Turkish Empire in the nineteenth century, the Hapsburgs and then the Hohenzollerns began that fateful Push to the East (*Drang nach Osten*) which was one of the main causes of the World War. The road down the Danube Valley led either through Belgrade and the valley of the Vardar to the Aegean or through Sofia and the passes of the Balkan Mountains, where the trains of the Oriental Railway climb slowly through from Bulgaria and then on to Thrace and Constantinople. But this, which is now the chief link between Central Europe and the Near East, is a development of recent years. Throughout the later Middle Ages and the early modern period it was Venice which held the primacy in the oriental trade with Western Europe while the Balkan countries remained isolated and backward. For people who live in history this greater past of Venice was still a vital fact in the peace settlement of 1919, and a continuing element in Italian-Yugoslav relations.

It was, therefore, a happy circumstance that the first lap of our journey to the Balkans started from Venice and followed its sea route down the Dalmatian coast. After a journey of two days and nights coasting along that historic background of ancient history, we had planned to turn inland to travel through Montenegro and southern Serbia before turning north to Belgrade and the valley of the Danube. It seemed a perfect plan, for in Montenegro we were to be met by the most distinguished prelate of Macedonia, Bishop Nicolai of Ochrida. One is tempted at the very first mention of the name of this remarkable man to pause and try to draw the portrait of one of the most unique personalities in Balkan history. But we must first get our bearings. Owing to the delay in my plans caused by the conference at Fasano and the breakdown of communication in Serbia, I was unable to get word through to Ochrida of the change in my timetable before the Bishop had left there to meet me at the coast. As is often the case, however, this initial failure turned out to be most fortunate, for it resulted in our traveling through Yugoslavia by both routes—that of the Adriatic and that from Belgrade down the valley of the Vardar and afterwards through Sofia to Constantinople.

It ought never to happen that a visit to Venice is an anticlimax, but after the Italian sunlight in the rich Po valley we found Venice veiled in misty rain, and even when the sky cleared in the evening the undefinable charm of that city which has no parallel in all the world was spoiled—I would almost say desecrated—by jostling crowds of German tourists filling the Piazza di San Marco, at whom the Italians looked askance in spite of the fact that they were spending black-market money freely in restaurants and shops. Even from the Grand Canal there were raucous sounds from the gondolas. We had seen the same kind of spectacle in Vienna at the very end of the war when the war profiteers (*Kriegsgewinner*) moved into the best hotels and restaurants, crowding out the old Viennese who had formerly been of the upper and middle class. For these were not representative Germans. Many of them came from Eastern Europe to exploit the disasters of Germany and Austria. It was largely a migration of racketeers, although the good Germans sadly admitted that some of their friends had been enticed by the chance of ready gain to join in the speculation in *valuta*.

The economic and social effects of war can last for many years, as the experience of our Southern States can testify, but we did not delay to study the situation in Venice, for it was only a way station for us. Our destination was across the Adriatic. Strangely enough we found little sign of any interest in Venetian tourist

circles in ships going along the routes of the old Venetian galleys.
We found this rather puzzling in view of the strength of Italian
feeling which had shown itself over Fiume, but Venice lives
largely by tourist traffic, and the tourists evidently preferred
traveling in Italy itself to the exploration of the Dalmatian coast.
In any case, by 1925 it was hard to find any information in Venice
about the way to reach the little seaports in the hidden bays
among the islands from Trieste to Ragusa. The Italian line, which
is the modern substitute for the Venetian galleys, sails from Trieste, rather than from Venice. But this line of express steamers
does not touch at the smaller ports, and we hunted up the Italian
postal and freight line that serves all coastal towns. The advertise-
ment stated that these boats sailed from Venice, but the ticket
offices and tourist agencies there knew nothing of them. After
much inquiry, their office—the Puglia Line—was at last found in
the Piazza di San Marco. But they sold no tickets there! Moreover, the boat for the weekend had already left before the ticket
office had been found, and it was necessary to take the day boat
over to Trieste to make connections with the coastal steamer
there.

This was the first time I had ever left Venice by sea. Just as the
domes and the sentinel-like Campanile were receding over the
horizon of marsh and lagoon, a fleet of Venetian fisher boats
drove up against our course. With bogue and orange sails like
those that Turner painted, with curving prow and stern, and
wide, shell-like sides, they cannot have changed much from the
time when galley slaves rowed them in the fleets of either Rome
or Venice.

The sea road to Trieste misses the interest of the railroad journey which passes along the southern end of the great battlefields
of the Karst region from Goritsia to the sea, which I had traveled
in previous years.

We arrived at Trieste just after dark, and at once took a carriage to find our way to the quay of the Puglia Line. Even in
Trieste it was not well known where these boats tied up; but

finally away beyond what seemed like miles of deserted wharves, we found the boat taking on its cargo. We were assured that all the cabins had already been taken and that there was nothing left for us but the open decks; but this proved to be our first contact with the kind of bargaining which is not uncommon in that part of the world. For a sufficient sum, they not only found a cabin for us, but the best cabin on the ship. Even this was rather primitive but not too bad, for the accommodations on the boat were approximately what one might find in a second class cabin on a Channel boat, if one would add to that an enormous pile of hides on the deck above, somewhat too late in their arrival for the tannery. However, with the aid of the baggageman, who turned out to be a Hungarian by birth and spoke French fairly well, we managed to make our quarters comfortable and had no further complaint on that score.

There was still time for an evening's exploration in Trieste. Our carriage took us past the enormous warehouses of the old Austrian Lloyd. Although it was early evening, there was not a sign of any living person inside the gates of the shipping yard, and no ships whatever along the wharf. Away over on a side pier one solitary boat was taking on coal, and that was the extent of the work being done that evening in the harbor of Trieste. On the other hand, if the streets showed little sign of commercial life, there was no indication of that abject poverty which fills the squares with beggars and street vendors. The Hotel de la Ville was crowded with tourist customers and the restaurants were well attended.

Trieste has lost all the political advantage which it had in Hapsburg times, and what is left there now is strictly due to the natural economic advantage of its situation. The fact that it remains an entrepôt with a steady dribble of commerce and travel from the north, as well as by the Adriatic, shows that there are still possibilities of revival. When the economic frontier lines of Europe become less barriers to trade than they are at present, Trieste may even regain its former importance on the Adriatic.

At sunrise we were steaming along a calm sea by the southern point of Istria, passing between the island Brioni and the mainland. Brioni is a pleasant, tree-clad island, entirely made over into an Austrian health resort in the times before the War. It is a sign of the recovery of Austria that Brioni is once more filled with its old-time guests.

Around a rugged point of coast and through a winding passage, we slipped into the still harbor of Pola, once the naval arsenal of the Hapsburg monarchy. That morning our mailboat was the only vessel in the harbor. As we neared the wharf there was not a sign of life, not even a pushcart on the deserted street. The town seemed almost as much a relic of the past as the great Roman amphitheater which arises almost from the water's edge. Before we touched the wharf, however, the siren of the naval arsenal echoed against the hillsides. A few workmen began to appear and a tram came groping around the corner. The Italian Admiralty apparently still had some use for the Austro-Hungarian equipment, but the old Roman amphitheater may once more become the most important asset of the city of Pola. However, a fine modern hotel beside it was mostly boarded up and the gardens around had grown wild. Just between the amphitheater and the wharf there was a solid block of stone with an inscription to Elizabeth, the murdered Austrian empress; but the statue itself was no longer there.

The amphitheater was the key to much that followed. Roman remains are of surprising extent in the Balkan countries. We came upon them again and again in the Dalmatian islands and seacoast, at Skoplje in old Serbia, and over the Danube into Rumania. The problems faced by the Romans in this part of the world were in some ways singularly like those of today, for the unity of the Roman Empire owed at least as much to the work of the engineer as to military power or administrative experience. The Roman roadmaker did for his day exactly what the modern engineer is doing to end the isolation of the Balkan states. The Roman sanitary engineer created for the cities of his day almost exactly the same water supplies as are being reconstructed now. For instance, Athens grown great once more in these postwar years digs out again the tunnels of Aurelian, in order to secure a sufficient supply of fresh water from the hills by Marathon. The reminder of ancient Rome was with us to the very close of our Balkan journey, when emerging from the Corinth Canal we saw the tablet of Nero at the western end, where his engineers had stopped their digging after two or three miles of excavation. An American engineer standing beside me on the deck of the steamer pointed back to the long straight cut of the modern canal and stated his belief that the Romans could have done it if they had had sufficient interest, economic or otherwise, to push it through. He was in charge of the work at Athens and said that the modern engineers had found that in every case the work of their Roman predecessors needed only to be restored and enlarged, that the engineering lines had been correctly drawn and the plans were as modern as those of today.

With such intelligence as this guiding the material work of antique civilization at its climax, with achievements like these fully as notable as the greatest of our time, one cannot but wonder what will be the ultimate fate of the so-called modern civilization. Cicero spoke in his day of "these modern times." There were at least two great evils in antique society which contributed to its destruction. In the first place, in spite of certain sanitary provisions and a tentative beginning of the science of medicine, there was a fatal decline in the population. In the second place, the economics of production were never on a sound basis owing to the fact that so much came in by way of tribute from the conquered. Both these causes of decline are largely due to a single underlying fallacy, which is summed up in the attitude towards war and peace. A predatory world could not develop its own production. Both life and property were cheap, so long as the supply came from the fruits of victory. This one underlying cause of the decline and fall of the ancient world could not be detected by the antique thinker because war was the basis of the whole structure of society, and to question its legitimacy would have seemed simply preaching anarchy. There was only one definite challenge of this kind, and that was in the teaching of Jesus. The Christian theology, however, was never as bold as the Gospels themselves, and as the Church grew and prospered in the temporal world, which had been built upon a philosophy which it implicitly denied, its mission as the champion of peace in this regard became almost negligible.

Strangely enough, in the twentieth century the problems of production and of peace have finally presented themselves in ways which admit of no equivocation. Alongside the science of economics, the product of the nineteenth century, the twentieth century is grappling with the parallel and not less vital issue of national security without war. There is no need to expect that repetition of historic cycles which envisages the destruction of the modern world as in the pages of Spengler's *Decline of the West*.

There was no time for developing these considerations in the harbor of Pola, for our postboat only stayed an hour at the wharf. Two or three vendors of local fruits sauntered down to the ship's gangway. The Italian mailbox was hung on the rail by the gangplank, and two or three letters were brought by hand and dropped into it. The total exchange of merchandise of a boat coming once every three days could almost be carried away on a wheelbarrow.

Nosing down beyond the Cape of Istria, we struck the rough waters of the Quarnero, the bay on the eastern side of Istria which runs northward up to Fiume. Our boat did not go to Fiume, but crossed the Quarnero southward to the Dalmatian islands. This was something like crossing the British Channel. Probably because of the mountain formation on the mainland, the north wind was always blowing strong and the waves ran high enough to toss the boat uncomfortably. Awnings were stretched along the north to shut off the spray.

We had expected to sail down the Dalmatian coast under the

blue skies always promised in the guidebooks; but instead, we met with mist and driving rain, low clouds, and almost colorless sea. Perhaps it was well that this was so, for we carried away no such enthusiastic memory of the beauties of the Dalmatian coast as one finds in all accounts of it. On the contrary, these islands, wind-swept and bare of any protection, showed all the ugliness of poverty, with an almost desperate lack of any resources for future development. The hillsides are almost like the ash-covered slopes of a volcano. In most rocky countries there is a contrast between the jutting cliff and green fields which makes the rock itself less formidable; but in the Karst region the dun-colored landscape is hardly more than the dust upon the rock, the rock itself being like a seared skeleton whose vertebrae, protruding from the sea, form the ridges of these long Dalmatian islands. There is little here in this poverty-stricken *Italia Irredenta* to attract settlers from Italy.

Yet as we sailed for two days and two nights along the channels between these islands from Trieste to the harbor of Ragusa (Dubrovnik), we found everywhere reminders of the empire of Venice and of the influence of the Italy of an earlier age still speaking daily from the architecture of the public buildings and the churches with their campaniles almost uniform in structure. There is no escaping history on the Dalmatian coast, for Venice left more than a memory of its century-long dominance, in the massive walls which protected its ports against invasion from the Turk, and in the delicate arcades along the open squares. All this is stretched out along the seacoast, leaving the Balkan interior almost untouched, for it is only rarely that there are signs of Venetian influence in the heart of the country where the Byzantine-Greeks recast the models of ancient Rome, and the Turks in turn made over the Byzantine architecture to their use. On the Adriatic shore it was the Venetians who took over the heritage of Rome, adding a lasting touch of grace and lightness to the massive walls of the Roman buildings. Even the republic of Ragusa, which throughout the centuries maintained its independence against both Venetians and Turks, preserved behind its walls, in monastery, church, and palace, and in its sunny square, the influence of medieval Italy.

As this opens a page of history seldom read nowadays, we may pause for a moment over it; just as, when night fell, we refreshed our memories from the guidebooks in the stuffy little cabin of the Puglia postboat. For, apart from its bearing on the problems of today, it is high romance in its own right.

The story of Venice begins with the barbarian invasions of the fifth century, when refugees from Goth and Hun hid away in little fishing villages on the sandbars by a swampy lagoon, near the mouth of the river Po. A hundred years before Charlemagne, these settlements united under a doge, and, with discipline at home and daring abroad, slowly but steadily planted trading posts along the Dalmatian coast, policing on their own behalf where Pompey had suppressed the pirates in Roman times. By the thirteenth century, Venice was the recognized queen of the Adriatic, tapping the caravan routes in Moslem bazaars and sending its goods to European markets. Its merchant princes, practicing the cynical philosophy of Machiavelli of a later day, used religion for the advantage of trade and politics, as when in 1202 they turned the Fourth Crusade aside from battling with the Moslem to the conquest of Venice's great rival in the Near East, Constantinople itself. From this time on Venice reaped both the chief profits from the trade of the Orient and the richest spoils of its art. The palaces of the merchant princes and the Cathedral of St. Mark were adorned with pillars and rarely colored stones, which Ruskin so much admired, robbed from the cities of Byzantium and the Levant, which in a still earlier age they had taken from other cities of long lost civilizations, in the recurring cycles of war. Supreme on the eastern Mediterranean after the defeat of its rival Genoa, in 1380, Venice gained rather than lost by the Turkish conquest of the Balkans when the empire of Stephen Dushan, the greatest of the Serbians of the Middle Ages, was overthrown at Kosovo in 1389. The monopoly of the sea routes then paid increasing dividends and the wealth of Venice became a byword throughout the West. Its six fleets numbered over 300 ships with crews of some 36,000 men. This was at a time when England was, as the Venetian merchant ambassadors noted, an isolated and crude country without art, literature, or good manners.

Then suddenly, at the opening of the sixteenth century, the sea route to India opened a new era for Europe, and Venice was doomed—at least as the metropolis of oriental trade. In 1502 when Vasco da Gama made his second voyage to India, Venice was only able to bring home a few pounds of spices—the richest product of its trade—and the foreign commerce of Europe shifted to Portugal and Spain and then to Holland, France, and England. Northern Europe rose from medieval backwardness into a new age of capitalist enterprise, and Venice ceased to play a great part in world affairs. But the memory of its past exploits still remained and stirred the fires of Italian nationalism, a sentiment made all the stronger by the fact that the lands of the Venetian Republic in northern Italy were the last to be regained from the Hapsburg occupation in 1866.

The recovery of the Venetian lands remained incomplete, however, both on the north and on the east, and when at the end of the First World War the hollow shell of the old Hapsburg monarchy was broken up, the slogan, *Italia Irredenta*, which had been the battle cry of earlier attacks on Austrian imperialism was renewed in a new and more vibrant form. The peace settlement at Paris readily assigned to Italy most of the Alpine Valley leading up the Alps to the Brenner Pass, but the claims to the Dalmatian coastline seemed unreal to European and American statesmen, who had forgotten or never known of the empire of Venice, claims that seemed doubly unreal because Venice itself seemed more like a museum of the past than a living metropolis of trade. Yet its empire, although strung out over the seas, had been even more definitely an Italian creation than the Roman Empire itself. For the Roman Empire was, after all, a cosmopolitan world and at its height had been ruled by men born on the far outskirts of the

Empire like Constantine, or on the Illyrian coast like Diocletian. Moreover, however much the Italians prided themselves as the heirs of Rome—a pride which Mussolini was not the first to exploit—the political links with the antique Empire were broken centuries ago. On the other hand, the Venetians, at least from the days of the Renaissance, were definitely modern Italians, and in spite of their lessened wealth their sea power still showed itself in the greatest naval battle since Actium, that of Lepanto in 1571, by which the Turks lost the mastery of the Mediterranean.

In contrast with this long and glorious history the kingdom of the Serbs, Croats, and Slovenes, which had only come into being at the Paris Peace Conference, seemed to Italians to be a mere upstart with no historical rights to Fiume, which had formerly belonged to Hungary, or to Zara, which was formerly Austrian. D'Annunzio's raid on Fiume turned out to be *opéra bouffe* but, while it alienated public opinion in other countries, it gave a romantic expression to a deep-seated Italian sentiment. In the final breakup of the Hapsburg monarchy it was felt that Italy, as an inheritor of the Venetian Empire, could at least assert the right to hold that strip of Dalmatian coast which the Austrians had seized in an act of pure imperialism when the Turks were driven out of the western Balkans. Italian writers pointed out in innumerable pamphlets and books the services which Venice had performed for the countries of Europe, when it took over the task, which Rome had once assigned to Pompey, of clearing out the pirates from the deep bays of the Illyrian coast. The Venetian settlements established at these ports had therefore been parts of a system of maritime police from which all Central and Western Europe benefited. On the other hand the Yugoslavs of the territories behind the coastline claimed that they had been chiefly responsible for the overthrow of the Turk and had been cheated of their inheritance by Austria and that therefore they had historic claims to outmatch those of Italy. Fortunately, most of these rival claims were settled at the Paris Peace Conference, but the sore remained open until finally a complete settlement was reached in the Treaty of Rapallo in 1920 by the statesmanship of Count Carlo Sforza, then, as now, Foreign Minister of Italy.

We arrived at Zara just at nightfall, the one Italian possession on the mainland. So much has been written of the picturesqueness of Zara that I had expected to find a city nestling against the Dalmatian mountains, but it is on a low, flat promontory jutting into the sea, and although along its wharf the medieval walls are still standing and its streets are narrow and intended for foot rather than for wheeled traffic, there was nothing outstanding in this city, except perhaps the fact of its general Italian character.

A night's sailing down the channels between the islands brought us at dawn into the harbor of Sebenico (Sibenik as it is called now). This harbor, with its long, narrow channel, is a smaller repetition of that of Pola. But here we were on Yugoslav soil, and a highway brought down the produce from the hinterland and piled it on wharves that were once more becoming busy. They were unloading enormous piles of iron ore along the wharf, and I learned by inquiry that the laborers represent a migration from the inland villages to the seacoast towns of Yugoslavia in the hope of finding work there. Their wages were only a few cents a day, and yet I had never seen men work harder than these mountain-bred Bosnian and Dalmatian workmen during the hours that our ship was tied up at this wharf.

Sebenico still lives in Venetian houses, but the life there is distinctly of the mainland, and the markets along the squares draw in a population absolutely distinct from that of an Italian market place. It at least is genuinely Dalmatian, although the cathedral is one of the most outstanding creations of Venetian art along the whole Adriatic coast.

By evening we were entering the harbor of Spalato (Split) in Yugoslavia, famous as the home of Diocletian, in which he spent the last years of his life close by the village where he was born. The half-ruined remains of his palace still form the center of the city, with alleyways and streets cut through palace rooms between slender columns of vaulted arcades. No palace of the Italian

Renaissance could compare in magnificence with this Balkan villa on the Adriatic seashore. Until Venetian days the entire city lay within the massive palace walls four stories high. For the palace was like a vast army camp nine to ten acres in size, with its four streets and four gates, one of which, the Golden Gate (*Porta Aurea*), although it now opens into the market place, still retains traces of its original dignity. In general plan the palace somewhat resembled the far greater magnificence of the forbidden palace at Peking. There were quarters for soldiers and officers of the Emperor, as well as the rooms actually occupied by him, when, after celebrating the last triumph that Rome ever beheld, he retired from his capital at Nicomedia, where he ruled the eastern half of the Empire from the Asiatic shore of the Dardanelles.

Until Venetian days the palace walls contained the entire city, and even now it lies mostly within them. It is at places like this, as at the Porta Negra of Trier on the Moselle, rather than in Italy itself, that the far reach of Roman power impresses the modern visitor. But nowhere else does history present such a commentary upon the transience of even that power as at Spalato, not so much in the ruins of the palace as in the fact that the cathedral is the mausoleum of the last great persecutor of the Christian Church. Under the dome of the tomb built for Diocletian, I heard the clergy of the Catholic archbishopric of Spalato chanting the vesper service. The baptistry, a perfect gem of architecture, was built as a temple of Jupiter.

Beside the northern gate is the medieval Venetian piazza with its loggia recalling that at Verona, but the rest of the square has left history behind, for it is arranged with the tables of Continental cafés. Spalato is making its bid to rival other Mediterranean watering places, and its spa, which drew Diocletian to choose this spot for his retirement, is being exploited again in the most modern way, with new communications to the hinterland. Fortunately the old city seems likely to be left more or less undisturbed, while new houses are being built out into the country on the northern side.

CORNER OF SPALATO, LOOKING
OM THE CATHEDRAL

SARAJEVO STREET SCENES

URKISH MOSQUE AND CHUSHAN, SARAJEVO

A night's sail brought us to Grovosa (Gruz), the port for the old walled city of Ragusa, now rechristened with its Yugoslav name, Dubrovnik, stretching down on a rocky point like a toy city beside a little bay. The walls still circle the town, with round towers and massive masonry protecting it against the Saracen raids and, on the landward side, crenelated and massive defenses against the Turk. There are few spots in Europe, or in the world, of such tranquil beauty, where history has lost all other tones than those of romance. Within the walls there is no wheeled traffic except little hand-pushed carts, although modern suburbs have grown up along the coastal hills. The day we arrived was perhaps the greatest in its history since the fleets of Venice crowded its harbor, for the King and Queen of Yugoslavia were to make their first entry into Ragusa that day. Along the whole length of the main street in the old town a crimson carpet was laid down for royalty to walk on. Gay streamers hung from balconies and windows, along with old rose or damask tapestries and oriental rugs. Garlands of flowers and laurel were hanging from the carts and walls, and peasants in gayest costumes from all over the countryside supplied life and movement to a pageantry such as I have never seen elsewhere.

We had hardly arrived before the prefect of the district came to call, stating that he had been instructed by his government in Belgrade to look after us during our stay in Ragusa. However, as he had the King and Queen on his hands that day, we did not trouble him with any problems. Next day we watched the royal procession; it was hardly in keeping with the magnificence of the setting, for modern royalty has the good sense not to dress in medieval costume.

The motor car which had been sent us from Belgrade was waiting for us and we were soon on our way south along the road to Cattaro and Montenegro where, we had been informed, we were to be met by Bishop Nicolai, coming overland from his see at Ochrida on the border of Macedonia.

The coast road turns inland after winding a mile or so along the cliffs, and then follows a *polje* or level river valley behind the first range of hills. The country is not carefully cultivated as in Italy, and we came upon the explanation for it later with our first glimpses of minarets. The Turk has left his mark upon this whole land. The peasant stock is just as sturdy as that of Italy, but there was no incentive to transform the valley and hillside into garden and vineyard beyond what was necessary for mere subsistence, because of the Turkish exploitation and corruption in government. This held true of all the Balkans down to our day.

The great surprise of the day came at the Bocca de Cattaro. This is a fjord to match the finest that Norway can produce. There is a perfectly marvelous drive for at least two hours along the sheer edge of the mountains, close by the water front, with ever changing glimpses of the mountain range behind, and islands with old churches on them that looked lonely behind their sheltering cedars and pines. Sometimes there were ruined towns whose walls still bear the mark of the fires that consumed them long ago. Finally, at the far end of the last great bay, several miles wide, we reached the city of Cattaro with the Lion of Venice on its walls, the ancient Church of San Trafano, and the city itself held tightly against the prong of the Montenegrin mountain barrier. Here we stayed for the night, resting for the morning's journey into Montenegro.

3 · The Balkans

IT WOULD BE HARD to find anywhere else in the world, not even in Switzerland, so perfect a natural frontier for a country as the massive mountain wall which divides the highlands of Montenegro from the Dalmatian coast. From the cloudy summit of the dark mountain Lovchen, which gave its name to the country and the people, it is claimed that one can look across the Adriatic to the far shores of Italy. This I was unable to verify because Lovchen remained hidden by the clouds whenever we were in its neighborhood. Anchored in this bastion on the Adriatic, the steep escarpment runs eastward to merge in the mountainous core of the Balkans, that reaches toward the Dinaric Alps in the north and to the southern chains, which turn eastward to Bulgaria and southward into Greece.

Behind this barrier which rose before us across the Bay of Cattaro lies another world than that of the Venetian coastal cities, each barred from the other by the mountains almost as definitely as the Rockies bar the inland access to California. Indeed in a small way—a very small way—the Dalmatian coast bears much the same relation to the back country as California does to the Rocky Mountain states and the Middle West. The chauffeur who drove us from Ragusa to Belgrade had tied at the side of the car a box of palms which grew in the sunshine of the Adriatic, to take it back as a souvenir of the sunshine and warmth of Ragusa. But if a few square miles of habitable soil on the Dalmatian coast would make Californians smile at the comparison, there was enough of vineyard and orchards, of olives, oranges, lemons, and figs, along with a milder Mediterranean climate, to make the people from the interior eager to assert a claim to that stretch of seacoast which, for the first time, was partly within their grasp.

One does not have to be more than a few days in the Balkans to realize that neither country nor people can be understood by viewing them in the present alone. They are still living largely in their own past. It is the penalty of isolation that it forces people to find in the deeds of their own ancestors that kind of interest in human affairs which modern peoples satisfy in their dealings one with another. Of all characteristics of Balkan life, this is supreme and outstanding. Shut off from Europe by impassable geographic as well as political barriers, each section of the country has held its few thousand people to the rigid contemplation of themselves. This is especially true of the Serbs, so long held under the rule of the Turk and so far removed from the hurried events of Western Europe. Their only journalist was the wandering minstrel who even now can hold for hours at a time the absorbed attention of these shepherds and farmers by telling the story of wars that happened long ago, reciting the narrative in long monotonous cadences ending in a slight touch of song and the rasp of a *gusla*, the horsehair violin.

When the Archduke Franz Ferdinand arrived in Sarajevo on the day before his murder, he may not have been aware of the fact that to the patriotic Serb of Bosnia as well as of Serbia proper it was more or less of a sacrilege to review the troops on the anniversary of the Battle of Kosovo in 1389 when the Serbs were defeated by the Turks and their independence destroyed. Although over five centuries had intervened, the chief Serbian paper of Sarajevo was not to be diverted even by the arrival of the Austrian crown prince from its annual remembrances of a day held sacred by the whole Serbian nation. Therefore the issue which appeared on the Archduke's breakfast table (if his functionaries ever permitted it to reach him) had its full front page bordered in black, a symbol of mourning for those fallen at Kosovo.

This remembrance of the past is kept alive in all kinds of symbolic ways. There is perhaps a touch of poetry in the claim that the Montenegrin cap, which resembles but differs from the Turkish fez, symbolizes in its red top, the blood spilt on the field of Kosovo, by its black braid and border, the mourning for the dead;

while the gold braid upon the crown points to the hope for the day of liberty, a day that came at Kumanovo in 1912 with the overthrow of the Turk, and again in the World War with the overthrow of the Hapsburg monarchy.

This persistence of the past in the outlook of the Balkan peoples may easily escape the western traveler where the villages preserve no buildings of antiquity and the countryside has been robbed of its monuments by invasion or a Turkish occupation. This is the case throughout most of the central Balkan peninsula. There are no feudal castles here as in Central Europe to remind one of the Middle Ages. Even the hills are bare from the deforestation carried out by Turkish governors in the effort to get rid of insurrection and banditry. The citadels that crown the heights of Belgrade and Sarajevo were built by the Turks themselves, and it is only in a few places like the ancient capital of the Czar Stephen Dushan at Üsküb, now Skoplje, that the ruined monuments of Serbian history have left their trace. That history, however, is by no means dead. It has remained engraved in the memory of a peasant people who even now, as the present begins to move with a disturbing swiftness, remain more conscious of the past than almost any other people of Europe.

This is not history, however, in our sense of the word. Imprisoned within the narrow confines of village life, it offers no clue to the great movement of events. No Balkan historian has ever written the history of the Turkish Empire, of which his country formed a part. For that matter no German or Austrian historian ever studied without prejudice the history and society of the southern Slavs and the other Balkan peoples themselves. But the fact remains that the only way to understand Southeastern Europe is by the gateway of history, neither legendary on the one side nor limited to the superficial narratives of war and diplomacy on the other. The political framework is necessary, but not sufficient. One has to know how the people themselves lived both under the Turk and north of the Danube. For Eastern Europe, varied in the extreme in custom as in costume, has one main characteristic: It is an agricultural world in which about 80 per cent of the population live and work on the land. The conditions of the lives of this peasantry were also largely similar, for nearly everywhere the old regime was that of the feudal ownership of large estates in which serfdom, once universal, was slowly giving way, although the great estates still lasted on. In Rumania almost half of the tillable soil was in the hands of some five thousand owners, representing about one-sixth of one per cent of the population. Further north in Poland the situation was perhaps even worse with estates of forty and fifty thousand acres. In Serbia and Bulgaria, however, the situation was different, for with the expulsion of the Turk and subsequently of the Austrians, the peasantry took over most of the land, working it in small holdings, 90 per cent of which were under twenty acres in size, and these included rough mountain land as well as the poljes or open fields scattered between rocky hillsides.

The social life of these Serbian peasants reflected this absolute democracy. Fortunately there was no need to create it anew, for throughout all of their long history of subjection to the foreigner, this country people, illiterate and isolated, had preserved, as the unit of their structural society, a patriarchal cooperative organization, the Zadruga (the word means "for fellow men"), held together by blood relationship and living and working together, sharing their tools and their marketing and even their amusements in games and dances. When the First World War began in 1914, it was claimed that over 90 per cent of the country people of Serbia belonged to Zadrugas of one kind or another, for as the country developed economically, the Zadrugas specialized into those handling credit, furnishing domestic supplies, or looking after the health and sanitation of their communities.

It was under these influences of home life, where all were equal, that this mountain folk maintained their unbroken spirit of independence, never admitting to themselves that the Turk or the Austrian could be their master; unlike most subject peoples, they never learned to cringe.

But while the roots of Yugoslav peasant democracy go back a thousand years, it was only at the end of the First World War in 1918 that the land laws of the new provinces of Yugoslavia were brought in line with those of Serbia and the land divided into holdings small enough so that no person could own more land than he could use himself. Then this property was guaranteed to the farmer by application of an old Serbian law which provided that no homestead—house, two oxen, and minimum land required for a family, with the tools to cultivate it—could be taken away from a farmer, nor could he alienate it by mortgage.

Conditions such as these were unknown north of the Danubian Valley but the land hunger was just as strong, if not stronger, and was one of the determining factors in the revolutionary era of Eastern Europe which followed the World War. For it was land hunger more than anything else which brought about the collapse of the old order of things in Russia. When the revolutionaries in 1917 told the peasants that they could go home and help themselves to the land, there was no way of keeping them any longer at the front. At the first suggestion that the land was henceforth to be their own, the peasant soldiers, afraid of being too late, abandoned the trenches and rushed home in a way reminiscent of a gold rush in America.

The Green International, as this peasant movement was termed in Southeastern Europe, has been well described in the opening pages of Dr. David Mitrany's volume on the economic and social history of the World War, *The Land and the Peasant in Roumania*, one of those rare volumes in economic history which will always remain a classic.

The process of breaking up and redistributing the estates was a tremendous task and especially difficult because the countries involved had no opportunity to prepare themselves for so sudden a change and no adequate staff to ensure an exact or just division of the land. In Yugoslavia, for instance, over two hundred thousand peasant families were provided with about nine hundred thousand acres of land. In Greater Rumania, including the new provinces of Bessarabia and Transylvania, some sixteen million acres were expropriated and distributed to the peasants.

These reforms were still going on in 1925. What their effect would be it was not yet possible to say. At first there was a lowered production in the agricultural output, although that may have been due in part to other causes at the end of the World War. But whatever the economic effects of the Green International, the hopes entertained in 1925 that it would be counted on to hold back the Red International proved illusory. The political cohesion of the independent peasantry proved to be less than that of communism, with its strict discipline and singleness of purpose. And yet the struggle between these two forces of freedom and collectivism in the vast rural world of Eastern Europe was only in the first chapter of a history which will probably extend throughout many future generations. For the dynamic forces created by industrialism will always have to reckon with the inborn desire to be master of one's own destiny. When that destiny is the repetition of the things held most worth while in a long past, ideals of freedom which it nourishes are too strong ever to be wholly rooted out. So long as the south and east of Europe remain predominantly agricultural Marxian Communism will be forced to make compromises with local custom. On the other hand, an anarchy of localism will have to yield more and more to social and economic controls and not be permitted to repeat the exploitation of a new industrial and capitalistic feudalism. The interplay of these two forces of freedom and social cohesion is bound to produce something different from either communism or unrestricted individual enterprise.

Whatever the future has in store, no one could travel through Southern and Eastern Europe in the unsettled years that followed the breakup of the great monarchies, without the feeling that social and agrarian reforms had been too long delayed. Almost everywhere, even where the soil was rich, the people themselves were living in poverty. The houses were small, even when the families were large, and although every self-respecting peasant had one good suit of clothes, and every woman one dress upon which she had lavished incredible industry combined with the utmost of good taste, their work-a-day clothes were only a little better than those of gypsies who lived at the very bottom of the social scale. Even in the heart of the Balkans, however, there was generally one house larger and higher than the rest, and in every case this was built by money sent home from immigrants to America or else was the proud possession of a returned immigrant himself. For in many cases almost the only free money in circulation was that which came from the mines of Pennsylvania, the lumber camps of Washington, or the slums of our great cities. Americans have little idea of the inspiration which these symbols of American wealth brought into the most isolated mountain valleys of Macedonia.

These great currents in the social life of Southeastern Europe are by no means all of the story, for the blood tie remains stronger than any economic motive as tribalism tends to dominate politics and to give a fighting edge to the new sense of nationalism. Balkan society therefore provided a unique laboratory for the social scientist, but it was an opportunity almost completely ignored, and the only descriptions of it were from Western visitors who viewed it with but casual or limited interest, generally concentrating upon some one nation as a special favorite. Prior to the World War it was the Greeks and Bulgars who profited most from this favoritism of Western students. It might have been expected that the Austrians in Vienna would have been interested in the history and social life of the Serbs, but few of them paid any attention even to the Croats or Slovenes, within the Hapsburg Empire itself. Behind this attitude lay the intellectual arrogance which prevented the Germans from ever understanding the Slavs. In Vienna I was warned by no less a philosopher and liberal thinker than Professor Wieser that the Yugoslavs could never manage their own affairs to create a civilization like that of Central Europe; that they would always be open to corruption and to faction, and that, although they could dream of great things to be done, they could never actually do them unless under the direction of the more advanced peoples of Central Europe. It was one of the enlightening results of my visit to find how utterly false this generalization proved to be. As a matter of fact, history was already proving that Germanic Europe had no right to look down upon the political capacity of the Slav. The Hapsburg monarchy, in spite of its long history, had never solved the fundamental problem of government, that of securing loyalty under freedom. Its ancient principle, "Divide and rule," had never put an equal accent on both verbs. It meant divide, in order to rule, and that, in turn, meant to rule the divisions of the Empire by keeping them properly subdued under a Germanic bureaucracy and an imperial army, and Magyar bureaucracies and armies, all of which centered in the imperial and royal guards and in the person of the emperor-king. There was no real experimentation in freedom from the days of Maria Theresa, when the feudal state began to be crystallized in the form which it retained to the very end.

The method of government that was necessary for Eastern Europe with its sectional and racial divisions was federalism, a device in government which no European country outside of Switzerland has ever fully appreciated or attempted. The dominant conception of government in Continental countries is that of power. This is even true of that leader in democracy and freedom, France. French liberalism differs from English and American liberalism in being chiefly negative, consisting of protests against and checks upon the exercise of power in the hands of government, rather than the positive policies of the parliamentary system of government which is based so largely upon compromise. The distinction between these two forms of government is fundamental, not only for the understanding of the problems of Southeastern Europe, but for the nations generally. When government is conceived in terms of power rather than of cooperation, opposition to it takes more or less of the nature of disloyalty if not of treason. Such a system of rule does not develop confidence upon the part of those not participating in its administration, and therefore tends to perpetuate and strengthen partisan divisions within the state. A little further thought makes clear the still more fundamental point that politics of power play into the hands of militarism and that militarism in turn has only respect for this type of government. It is certainly not because of any superior political capacity upon the part of the British or American peoples that they have subordinated militarism in both law and practice. It is because of their freedom from the continuing menace of invading enemies. Continental Europe has all along been limited in its method of government by its insecurity from war. International peace is an essential not only for the development of freedom but also for efficiency in government.

These basic principles of political science lie in the forefront of any study of the three great empires which were destroyed by the revolutionary impact of the World War of 1914–18. But they were equally evident in the history of Yugoslavia, the official title of which, "The Kingdom of the Serbs, Croats, and Slovenes," bears on the face of it the challenge to create a federal state. Instead of that, however, the Serbs insisted upon a unitary form of government at Belgrade in which they could dominate. We were soon to see the discord which this refusal of federalism was to bring about. But no one then could have imagined that the time would come when the dragon's teeth sown by this refusal to grant local autonomy to Croatia would help to bring about the completely opposite situation in which a Croatian despot would rule at Belgrade with ruthless disregard of the old local liberties of the Serbs themselves.

In 1925 the making of this history had only begun and this is not the place to develop further the long range consequences of the failure of federalism in the Near East. But the shadow of coming events was already slowly darkening the horizon in both Belgrade and Zagreb, as the later narrative will show.

The problems of Southeastern Europe are only partly explained, however, by a survey of its present-day adjustments to the conditions of life in the twentieth century. However, more than anywhere else the drama of the present is here determined by that of the past, and nowhere else is that drama less studied by the outside world. Down to the breakup of the Turkish Empire it was commonly believed that the liberated countries would always be obliged to follow the policies of the major powers. History was to disprove this concept which lay behind European politics and diplomacy for the decline of the Turkish Empire left, not a vacuum, as historians wrongly designated it, but an area of discord with a constant menace of mountain feud, trouble or national war. Yet no serious or sustained effort was made to lessen the animosities cherished from past wars or nourished by present provinces, except by partisans of this or that country. In England, ever since Gladstone challenged public opinion by his attack upon "the Bulgarian atrocities," there had been a pro-Bulgarian movement in liberal quarters. There was also a traditional English friendship for Greece from the days of the Greek War of Independence, a century before. But there was little appreciation of the character of the people of Serbia, and when in the First World War the Serbians, at the decisive Battle of Kumanovo, and then again in the Second Balkan War joined with Greeks to overthrow the Bulgarians, the great powers found themselves faced with a new and completely unforeseen situation. It was Serbia which had gained most, especially in the age-old disputed territory of Macedonia, and it was this fact which lay behind the Austrian ultimatum against Serbia after the assassination of the Archduke Franz Ferdinand on June 28, 1914.

Behind these events of recent times lies a great chapter of history almost unknown in the West, that of the rise and decline of the Turkish Empire in Europe. Our school manuals give little hint of the fact that in Martin Luther's day, when the national state was just taking final form in England and France, and the Holy Roman Empire was approaching eclipse, the Ottoman Turk extended his boundaries to the walls of Venice on the west and India on the east and held the Black Sea as a Turkish lake by the conquest of southern Russia. It was not only a land empire, for his fleets ranged the Mediterranean until, in the Battle of Lepanto in 1571, Don Juan of Austria, with papal and Venetian aid, won a sea fight over the Turks which was one of the decisive battles of history. In the valley of the Danube the frontier moved backward and forward with the fortunes of war and it was not until the nineteenth century that the decline of the Turkish Empire in Europe definitely began.

The first notable blow was struck by the uprising of the Serbs in 1804 under Karageorge (Black George), a peasant leader and former swineherd, in whose family the supreme command of the Serbian troops was made hereditary. But in 1812, when Napoleon invaded Russia which had been the protector of the Serbs, Alexander made peace with Turkey and allowed the Turkish army to reconquer Serbia. Four years later, however, another Serbian leader, Milosh Obrenovich, forced the Sultan to acknowledge the autonomy of Serbia. Milosh and his sons ruled Serbia until 1842 when, by a military revolt, the son of Karageorge was brought back, only to be dethroned again in 1858 by the old Prince Milosh and the house of Obrenovich ruled until 1903. Then by a military conspiracy King Alexander and Queen Draga were assassinated and Prince Peter of the house of Karageorge was brought back as king. Under his son, Alexander, Serbia fought through the First World War and ended as the dominant partner in Yugoslavia. But tragedy continued to stalk Serbian royalty and Alexander himself was assassinated at Marseilles in October, 1934.

The liberation of Greece was a simpler story for, from the Greek War of Independence in 1820–29, the Turks never regained sovereignty in the peninsula. The same treaty of Adrianople which had recognized the independence of Greece in 1829 secured practical independence from the Turks for the two principalities north of the Danube River, Moldavia and Wallachia, which in 1862 were united under the new name Rumania.

In spite of his declining power, the Sultan still held the Central

Balkans throughout the rest of the nineteenth century, chiefly by playing off one great power against another. In 1875, however, it seemed for a time as though the final movement of emancipation of the Balkan peoples from the Turks had really come when insurrection broke out in Bosnia and Herzegovina and spread in the following year from Montenegro and Serbia to Bulgaria. In Bulgaria the insurrection was suppressed so brutally by Turkish irregular troops that Gladstone was stirred to protest in the British Parliament, and Russia began preparation for war. But in the western Balkans the Serbs and Montenegrins who had boldly declared war on the Sultan were left to themselves and utterly defeated. Then in the peace settlement not they but Austria-Hungary profited most, for it was at the Congress of Berlin that Austria was given its mandate to occupy Bosnia and Herzegovina and to garrison a strip of territory lying between Serbia and Montenegro known as the Sanjak of Novi Bazar. Both Serbia and Montenegro were rewarded for their heroism by being reduced in territory while Austria which had risked nothing gained most. The hope cherished by many Serbs for a greater Serbia was thus frustrated, and, when finally in 1908 Austria-Hungary annexed Bosnia and Herzegovina, profiting from the fall of the Turkish Empire, there was a passionate Serbian outcry for war against the Dual Monarchy. Peace was, however, preserved by Nicola Pashitch, whose strong hand guided Serbia through most of its history from 1904 through the World War and the formation of the new kingdom of Yugoslavia. Pashitch's pacific policies of 1908 were perhaps chiefly due to the fact that the Russian Government "advised" giving up all claim to territorial expansion and leaving the Balkan question for solution by the great powers. But in 1914 the initiative among the great powers was taken by Austria, and there was no way of stopping war when Germany gave its consent.

The year 1908 also witnessed the Young Turk Revolution which transformed the sultanate into a modern state under Kemal Pasha, but this great reform in Turkey itself was carried out by nationalists who proceeded to alienate the subject or associated races. The result in European Turkey was the formation of the Balkan League of 1912 for the final liberation of the Balkans from Turkish rule. Venizelos, the most distinguished statesman of modern Greece, got most of the credit for the formation of this league, but it was really begun by the Bulgarian Gueschoff. He has told the story in an autobiography which, unfortunately, few people have read. The first to lead the attack was Montenegro, and then the Bulgarians, Serbs, and Greeks joined in and quickly and decisively defeated the Turks—the Bulgars at Kirk Kilissa and the Serbs two days later at Kumanovo. The great powers were completely taken by surprise and the old diplomats were aghast at this sudden collapse of the Turkish Empire. At Sir Edward Grey's suggestion an armistice was drawn up to keep the Bulgarian armies out of Constantinople and a London conference was called to do for the Balkan League in 1912 what the Berlin conference did for the earlier one. The conference seemed at first about to succeed, but was suddenly halted when the Bulgars attacked their late allies the Serbs and the Greeks. It was this Second Balkan War of 1913 in which so many atrocities were committed that the Carnegie Endowment sent its mission to investigate.

The final settlement by the Treaty of Bucharest (1913) attempted to draw the boundaries of the Danubian states, but for peasant people to whom land means everything and whose roots of family and clan have been deep in the soil for centuries the tracing of a frontier is the most serious thing in life. It was therefore almost unavoidable that the mountaineers of Macedonia who found their country divided up among the three neighboring states with no recognition of their own autonomy should continue to make trouble, especially when the neighboring states themselves cherished continued animosities from their war.

This was the condition of affairs which brought the crisis of 1925 in which the League of Nations saved Europe from a third Balkan war—an incident that occurred when I was in Bulgaria itself.

4 · From Montenegro to Belgrade

FROM CATTARO the road winds up the sheer face of the mountain wall. The previous afternoon, while motoring along the shore of the bay, we had seen the white ribbon of its zigzagging course from miles away and could not believe that this could be the one main roadway from the north to the uplands of Montenegro. The actual climb was equally disconcerting, as the car backed on each turn only a few feet from the steep edge. The mountain itself was dark and sinister, but as we neared the top of the pass, was lost in mists which soon blurred out the lowlands as well. But on our way back the clouds lifted, so that we saw what Baedeker properly describes as one of the few most remarkable sights in all Europe, the wide-spreading Bocca de Cattaro on the north and the Adriatic to the west, over which, with a little help from the imagination, one could see the dim line of the Italian coast.

The mist turned into a heavy rain as we crossed the mountain pass into Montenegro, and it continued raining all that day. When we arrived in Cetinje we learned that Bishop Nicolai had come all the way from Macedonia to meet us but had already left again, having heard the false report that we were not coming to Montenegro but had turned east from Ragusa to Sarajevo. However, the Governor of Montenegro at once got busy with telephone and telegraph, explaining our delay to the Bishop and the impossibility of reaching him by a message while he was traveling through the mountains; the Archbishop, who also is the Metropolitan, insisted upon our being his guests in his "monastic" palace. It was a pleasant and a comfortable house, but the one thing that both of us noticed was a large grapevine by the side of the house which made us feel at home at once, for it was a Concord vine loaded with its blue clusters of grapes, the only Concord grapevine I have ever seen outside of America. The Archbishop told us that it had been given him by a lady from New England and had prospered from the first, for apparently the climate of Montenegro exactly matches that of New Hampshire. The Archbishop also had as guest a very interesting person who knew all about our coming and who energetically took charge of much of our journey from Cetinje to Belgrade, Mme Helen Lazarovitch. I was never quite sure of the extent of her official connections in Belgrade, but speaking good French, she served as interpreter and explained with great intelligence and untiring courtesy every interesting point along the way.

The next day we went on into the heart of Montenegro, down the road that leads southeasterly from Lake Scutari, 1,000 feet up the long river valley of Podgoritsa, and beyond that to Danilovgrad, to an orphanage situated on the edge of high mountains. It had been begun by the American Red Cross during the war, and that was why I was taken to look at it. I have seen many traces of American charity in Europe in various countries, but never anything quite so touching as this lonely institution, where six years after the war over one hundred war orphans were being given the rudiments of schooling along with what one might call the rudiments of food and clothing, for they were not more than that. The local authorities could give little support to maintain the school, for it was a poverty-stricken mountain community. The huts were falling in ruins, the rain was coming through the roofs, the wind blowing through the broken sashes of the windows. There was no material for repairs, but in the warehouse there were still some blankets and clothing, warmer and better I suppose than many a village for miles around could afford. This was the only institution of its kind which I had time to visit here, but I was told that there are some traces of our Red Cross and relief work in practically every section of the country where it was most needed. If we were only able to act constructively in international politics as we have in international philanthropy!

Our visit to Montenegro was an eye opener from more than one angle. The Montenegrin people made the impression upon us of a most attractive nation. Even the poorest of them, and that means most people, have a quiet dignity in bearing and a reserve in manner which is to some extent shared by all European peasantry and especially by those who live in the mountains. But the Montenegrin, however poorly clad, looks as though he were always conscious of the way in which his people maintained themselves against the Turk throughout history. And the women are, if anything, more than a match for the men. On social occasions, such as the tea they gave for us, they wear their national costume which is by far the most graceful and becoming of all those we saw; a black velvet bolero over a white waist embroidered in gold, or a three-quarter length robin's-egg coat over a black skirt makes a handsome combination—not overdone but with the same suggestion of reserve as in their bearing. The women braid their hair and wear it like a crown, with a black mantilla hanging down the back.

While one frequently sees armed peasants along the roadside, the guns are for hunting, not for use in mountain feuds, for the country now is peaceful, and the Montenegrins have accepted unification with Serbia with very little dissent—all of which makes them very popular in the rest of the country.

We were just a few days late to see the ceremonial welcome of the King and Queen on their first official visit to Montenegro. Had we known of this in Geneva we might have arranged our north Italian trip so as to be in Cetinje in time. For after we arrived we found that we had been invited to sit at the royal table at the great open air banquet, where over a thousand mountaineers, dressed in their picturesque costumes, sat down to dine with the King in the park of the palace of the former King Nicholas.

That would have been a wonderful experience, but nothing as

compared with what followed when the whole assembly crossed the first mountain range from Cetinje over to the very top of Lovchen (Monte-Negro) and carried to the summit the remains of their most famous poet, "Prince" Njegosh, who is perhaps the greatest single hero for both Serbia and Montenegro in the whole modern period. By his own request Njegosh had been buried on the mountaintop when he died in 1856, but the Austrians had removed the body to Cetinje to make room, as it was believed, for some great Hapsburg monument of victory. Both the King and the Queen climbed to the very pinnacle of the mountain and the ceremony was one that impressed the imagination of the whole country.

I was struck by the fact that the portrait of Njegosh hangs in a place of honor in the Aula of the University of Belgrade, and when one takes that fact along with the way in which a group of ragged peasants in Montenegro tried to explain to us how much they revered their greatest poet, one gets an idea of the hidden forces of union which cement the two branches of the Serbian peoples.

We came back by the same road to Ragusa (Dubrovnik), for that was our only way to Sarajevo. We hurried across the barren stretches of Herzegovina, along the river valley, the only fertile part in many miles of motoring. For in this, the Karst region, with its rocky outcroppings and poor soil, the corn is sickly and the herds of cattle correspondingly poor. By noon we had left all traces of the Mediterranean world behind and were entering Moslem territory at the old Turkish town of Mostar, with its mosque and minaret and the old high bridge which spans the Narenta with an arch so high that crossing the bridge is like going over a small-sized hill.

From Mostar to Sarajevo we had to pass over the Dinaric Alps which divide the inland country of Bosnia from Herzegovina. The road lay over a pass some 3,000 feet high, and as we climbed into the clouds night came on, the blackest of nights completely enveloping us in cloud and rain. The road was as rough as a quarry road with holes filled with mud up to the hubs, and our lights all but went out every time we slowed down. But our Berliet plugged ahead and George, our Russian chauffeur, mended tires when necessary, and although we lost our way more than once, and the Bosnian peasants could not understand Russian Serbian, we managed somehow to reach Sarajevo before midnight and were comfortably lodged in the Hotel de l'Europe.

Sarajevo is, more than any other place that I know, the meeting place of East and West. One half of the town is as modern as Vienna—broad streets and impressive blocks of buildings. The other half is utterly Moslem with bazaars instead of shops, veiled women on the streets, and men thronging the mosques at the hour of prayer.

The afternoon of the next day I found that the main dining room of the one European hotel in Sarajevo had been formed into a private room for our reception. The Governor of the district presided and with him was the Mayor of the town, the Commanding General of that section of Bosnia, the Metropolitan and the leading members of his clergy, the Chief Teacher in the Seminaries, the heads of the cultural societies under whose auspices the "tea" was given. I was introduced by the Governor, and then spoke at some length on "Problems of Constructive Peace" indicating the line of work that the Carnegie Endowment undertakes throughout the world and the kind of work which it approves of even when it is not in a position to collaborate. The lecture was translated for me by Mme Lazarovitch, whom I felt I could fully trust; and yet I had the feeling here as on every other occasion when I spoke in the other Balkan centers that single visits of this kind could not do more than raise questions in the minds of the listeners which could not be answered without months or years of study and personal contact with those in other countries who were facing the same problems in the same way.

It struck me at the time as one of the strangest of chances that

I should begin my work in the Balkans by speaking to the citizens of the city of Sarajevo. The murder of Archduke Franz Ferdinand was still in every mind, and the two leaders of the societies under whose auspices I spoke had both been tried by the Austrians on the charge of complicity in the murder but had escaped on a technicality. They had been then propagandists for Bosnian union with Serbia, and their societies are the societies for spreading Serbian culture in Bosnia. It was Mme Lazarovitch who gave me the first satisfactory explanation of their part in the conspiracy. They were young intellectuals whose imaginations had been fired by the victories of the Serbs in the Balkan Wars and who shared the same kind of irritation against the Austrian bureaucracy that was to be found in every non-Germanic section of the Hapsburg monarchy. Their reading, however, had been mainly in Russian literature and history, and it was therefore natural under the circumstances that they accepted the doctrine of Russian terrorism, which by striking at the head of the government sought to effect revolutionary changes with the least possible bloodshed. This paradox seems strange to Western thinking, but unless one understands it and the basis for it, there is little chance of understanding the Balkans and Eastern Europe. In the Balkans it fitted in naturally with the persistence of feuds among people still living in a partially tribal society. It was clear that in their minds, and I imagine in the minds of most Balkan peoples outside, as well as inside, Serbia the theory of assassination of tyrants was fully accepted.

The young women I met, who had also been in the conspiracy, were devoting their lives unselfishly to a movement in adult education. Through an organization called Prosveta both men and women were engaged upon a struggle with illiteracy in the back country of Bosnia as well as in the towns. It was also part of the nationalist movement, but not in a narrow sense, because they had translated into Serbian some of the classics of Western literature as well as Russian and were printing them in cheap pamphlets for distribution in local libraries and homes. I examined their plant and looked into some of their libraries and could hardly believe that so much could be done with so little.

It was under these auspices that I gave my first lecture in the Balkans. The theme of my talk was geared as closely as possible to the situation. For the one argument for peace which they could understand was based upon history. The long Turkish occupation lay behind them, with its denial of freedom throughout the centuries under a military caste. Then came the occupation of the Austrian, with an effort at betterment but an almost equal failure to understand, because of the rigidity of bureaucratic rule and the constant threat of military action. Then, finally, as a result of the World War came the opportunity to build a different kind of civilization.

The next day was Friday and the bazaars were closed, but the mosque was crowded with worshipers, and rich and poor stopped on the sidewalk to take off their shoes as they entered the place of prayer. I learned later what should have been obvious then, that the people on frontiers of Mohammedanism in the Balkans are far more orthodox and deeply religious than in cosmopolitan centers like Constantinople. Here West and East, Europe and Asia, actually met face to face. In Metternich's day the saying in Vienna was that "Asia begins at the Landstrasse," the eastern end of that splendid boulevard which replaced the medieval walls of that city which throughout all European history had stood on the frontiers of the Germanic world. But this was no figure of speech in Sarajevo, where the modern Franzjosefsgasse ends not in a university, as at Vienna, but at a mosque, one of many whose domes and slender minarets sprinkle the Slavic quarter of lattice-windowed houses. The Franzjosefsgasse itself is a provincial, pretentious copy of the great street in the capital; but, leading off from it, tortuous alleyways, left untouched by the builders of the Austrian section of the city, wind down toward the river to the native coffee houses, where the music is not that of the Viennese opera but the plaintive wailing notes of the wandering minstrel's one-string violin or tremulous flute, the accompaniment to some ballad of the far-off days of Stephen Dushan of the fourteenth century, the last of the Serbian Czars.

That reminds me of a story that the Serbian Minister, M. Myatovitch, told me in London in 1904. He was an old man then, with a rich store of reminiscences from the political life of the nineteenth century. As a young man he had studied at Oxford, having been sent to England on a scholarship, and he heard Gladstone speak in the House of Commons. He said that nothing else in his long career in politics ever made such an impression upon him as Gladstone's eloquence in parliamentary debate. He went back to Belgrade and became Minister of Finance and made a budget speech in which he copied Gladstone as far as he could. But his ministry was overthrown that very night, and the King sent for him to console him at a quiet little dinner with just the two of them. Before it was over, however, they heard through the open windows the *gusla* minstrels in the street singing about the fall of the ministry. The King turned smiling to Myatovitch and reminded him of the difference between the age of the troubadours and that of Gladstone. There are now evening papers in the streets of Belgrade, but the minstrels are still the journalists of the Serbian villages.

As we left Sarajevo, the morning mists were still hung low over the mountains, but they cleared away before we reached the dark forest belt of pine trees which covers all the hills of this part of Bosnia. There were gypsy encampments along the roadside from time to time, a reminder of the fact that gypsies form a relatively large part of the inhabitants of the more backward areas throughout all the Balkans. The Bosnians themselves live in villages of little, square, steep-roofed thatched huts, clustered together for company and protection. The contrast between the homes of these peasants and the great government buildings in Sarajevo was an object lesson in misgovernment. For some distance, it was still Moslem country, as was evident from the dress of the men and women at a fair in one of the mountain towns. All of this country is upland, with a long descent to the River Drina, which separates Bosnia from the western boundary of Serbia. Just before crossing the ferry at Zvornik we had dinner in an old-fashioned Turkish hotel. Then we crossed the swiftly flowing river into Serbia and began the next stage of our journey along a pleasant river road.

The contrast between Bosnia and Serbia was striking. Here almost all the cottages were new, and looked recently white-washed. Apparently they had been rebuilt by the Serbian Govern-ment to replace the devastation of the Austrian army; for it was at Sabac in this extreme northwestern corner of Serbia that the Austrian army crossed the Sava River for the invasion in August, 1914. The countryside, apparently of rich alluvial soil, looked more prosperous than anything we had seen since we left West-ern Europe. There were almost continuous corn fields, with long villages stretching by the roadside. Sabac itself, a large border town of some ten thousand inhabitants, had a good hotel which had a modern touch, partly due to the fact that its proprietor had lived fourteen years in America.

The road from Sabac, which ran part of the way along the Sava River, was strangely enough the very worst we found in all the Balkans. For almost one hundred kilometers there was nothing but deep mud with pit holes in the ruts. There seemed to be no good reason why the Serbian Government had not repaired this one trunk road running west from Belgrade, unless, as someone suggested, it was to keep connections as poor as possible with Croatia and other non-Serbian portions of Yugoslavia. The peas-ants, however, were having gay times at more than one village. There were wedding parties, with dances on the green, the music supplied by swarthy gypsies. Even along the road, we met one procession of country wagons, with the musicians playing in each cart.

At the town of Obrenovac, where we had dinner, they were holding a country fair—with a horse race of peasant horses which they insisted were partly of English breed. The Governor of the district met us here with further word from Bishop Nicolai, who, learning that we were not coming across southern Serbia, was on his way to meet us in Belgrade.

Late in the afternoon, the road wound up a sloping hill with a view over the rich farming country to the southern far-off peak of Avala, famous in fable and history, and now the site of the tomb of the Unknown Soldier. Then, ahead of us in the distance on the east, we saw at last the citadel and the widely spreading houses of the city of Belgrade.

5 · Belgrade

F EW CAPITAL CITIES can rival Belgrade in magnificence of situation. At the point where two great rivers meet, the Sava from the west and the Danube from the north, a steep bluff rises two hundred feet to the ancient walls and towers which in the Middle Ages gave to the city its name of the white castle (Biograd or Beograd, in Serbian). The citadel, now no longer used as a fortress, has weathered to a dull maroon in color, but the marks of age are fitting in a spot so reminiscent of the history of the Near East. Archaeological excavations have shown that the Celts fortified the site before the Romans built their *castrum* in what later became the castle yards. Throughout the Middle Ages the citadel was held in turn by the invaders and defenders of the Roman Empire. Charlemagne's Frankish troops reached this far east and Bulgarians, Greeks, and Hungarians held it at times, as well as the Serbs themselves. Then through still more centuries it was a prize of war between Austrians and Turks, and it was not until 1867 that the last Turkish garrison left this frontier post of their diminishing empire. Some of the old red-roofed Turkish houses are still to be seen in the lower parts of the town, but there is little sign of the past in the section that stretches out from the gardens on the south slope of the citadel, with a modern boulevard copying those of Paris and Vienna, cosmopolitan hotels, and busy shopping crowds.

But one does not go far to find the touch of the Balkans, sometimes as subtle as in Vienna or Bucharest where the gypsies play mixtures of Western music and Balkan folksongs. In Belgrade, however, there are fewer variations on Western tunes, especially in those cafés frequented by countryfolk. Still more distinctive is the dress of these peasants crowding in the market place and along the side streets toward the lower town. In these quarters the dull clothes of the townsfolk are outmatched by the bright colors in buttons or ribbons on men's square-cut linen clothes and women's quilted petticoats and white or yellow kerchiefs tied under the chin. Mingling with the Serbs are Magyar horsemen and Croats with wide-brimmed hats, for each section of the country keeps its distinctive dress. Jostled through this crowd, one feels even more than in the provincial city of Sarajevo the sense of an ancient frontier guarding its history in the stubborn folkways of a semitribal world.

We had only glimpses of these aspects of Belgrade as we drove to our thoroughly modern hotel on the boulevard. Our rooms were at the top, looking out over the gardens of the royal palace and the roofs of the city to the great plain across the Danube, which here swells out to a miniature lake, almost like the mid-Hudson. The land to the north was Hungary until the Paris Peace Conference moved the frontiers of Yugoslavia across the river to include territory that had been colonized by the Serbs three hundred years before. For when the Emperor Leopold was engaged in the heavy task of driving the Turks back across the Danube he invited Serbian settlers from the hill country into the rich farmland of the plain. It was here that one of the greatest of American scientists was born, Michael Pupin, who has left an unforgettable picture of his boyhood home in his autobiography, *From Immigrant to Inventor*. The shift of the Hungarian frontier both here and in the Banat to the east gave Serbia provinces of richer farmland than could be found almost anywhere in the hill country to the south. Yet it was the Hapsburg himself who had brought the Serbs over the Danube into this rich farmland. Immediately in front of our windows, however, there was a reminder of another and more tragic chapter of Serbian history, for we looked out on the upper stories of the old royal palace and down into the garden from which the conspirators attacked the palace that night in 1903 when King Alexander and Queen Draga and their palace attendants were slain. It is strange how the memory of a crime haunts a spot. Although the old palace was not torn down, a new one was built just across the street where the present King and Queen can live unhaunted by any ghosts. But apparently they both prefer their country estate some distance out from the city. More monumental than the royal buildings, however, is the new Parliament building to the east, also in view from the windows. It looks like an American state house of the better sort in almost any of our state capitals. There is the big dome in the center and the little ones on the wings and a formal line of great pillars with Corinthian capitals set along the upper steps of the main entrance.

We did not have much time to get our bearings, for at last we found Bishop Nicolai who had done his best to meet us on our way. Tall and dark, with flowing beard and jeweled cross above his long clerical coat, he was very much an ecclesiastic and bore himself on all occasions with a quiet dignity. But more than dress or manner, one felt the presence of a great personality, kindly but forceful, and as we verified on many occasions, saintly and unworldly yet capable and efficient. It was not long before one could understand why he had refused the highest office in the Serbian Church, that of Patriarch, and chose instead the bishopric of Ochrida in Macedonia, the poorest in the land. Disgruntled government officials told us later how he had refused to accept government subsidies for his own use and had turned the money over to the rebuilding of his church. Later on we were to see more of this strange mixture of apostolic poverty and episcopal dignity, of practical management of affairs and a mysticism which led him to spend part of each year in seclusion with the Black Monks of Athos. As a contrast to this it was interesting to see that the Bishop brought along, to serve as interpreter, a priest slightly younger than himself, about forty years old, who had studied in Cambridge. His English was no better than that of the Bishop, but apparently interpreting was beneath the latter's dignity, at least on certain occasions. This seemed a little strange to us because the Bishop was known in London for the eloquence of his English sermons, but we learned later on that ecclesiastical

dignitaries in this part of the world are expected to maintain state in a manner second only to royalty, and this the Bishop did on occasion.

The first day in Belgrade was mainly given over to receiving callers, of whom there was a continual stream. The Rector of the University, Paul Popovitch, came to arrange my lectures there. Another visitor was Dr. Kojac, the head of the Health Zadrugas or Cooperatives, which I was very anxious to study because of Dr. Kingsbury's work with them when he was in Serbia as head of the Red Cross. Then there was the head of the Anglo-Yugoslav Club and the YMCA, both arranging for talks to their organizations. At the end of the day we had dinner in our room—just the three of us—and it was the best the hotel could supply. The good Bishop enjoyed it in an absent-minded way.

But there was nothing absent-minded about his planning for our trip. As much as possible this was to be under the auspices of the Orthodox Church, or at least to have its official sanction. Therefore our very first formal visit was to be with the Patriarch or Metropolitan of Yugoslavia at his official seat at Karlowitz in Slavonia, about forty miles up the Danube from Belgrade. This plan threw light upon the previous effort of Bishop Nicolai to be the first to meet us when we arrived in Montenegro. Nothing was said to link together the two plans of the Bishop and there may not have been any connection between them, but the Orthodox Church had played a great role in the past and was on the watch for the maintenance and assertion of its place in the new states which had been carved out of the Turkish monarchy. The result was that it became involved in the peculiar quality of Balkan politics and largely sacrificed its moral influence thereby. This has been particularly true of the higher clergy, who, with notable exceptions like Bishop Nicolai, have been mostly subservient to the existing political regime. The capacity for moral leadership, however, is by no means lacking, although it takes a different form from in the West. The spiritually minded turn to solitary contemplation in monasteries rather than to the preaching of reform, although Bishop Nicolai does both. Because I had already known of his unique position in this regard I was, therefore, glad to follow his advice and to begin work next morning with the visit to the Patriarch. This was to be by auto, but before the evening was over the Secretary of the Foreign Ministry called, presented his compliments, and left us railway passes to travel over Serbia. Over coffee, he proved to be a famous poet from Mostar. Apparently, from the Bishop's attitude toward him, he was not a Moslem. Yet if there ever was a Turkish looking city, it was Mostar.

The road to Karlowitz led down the hill of Belgrade and over the river to the rolling northern plain, with its many vineyards. At Karlowitz, a small country town, the cathedral was not impressive, a baroque building of the late eighteenth century, but the palace and library of the Patriarch were extensive. The Patriarch himself had been newly appointed, but though he owed his place to Bishop Nicolai's refusal to accept the office, he maintained that slight touch of conscious authority in the presence of the other ecclesiastics which gave a formal tone to the relationship of the two men. The Bishop, however, arranged it so that we had several hours' discussion of the European situation as well as of the immediate purpose of my visit, and it was soon evident that the Patriarch was well up on political matters. The dinner was formal enough to give it an official touch which, it was evident, Bishop Nicolai had expected. We stayed overnight as the Patriarch's guests and at his request gave a "conference" on the problems of war and peace, which was attended not only by the clergy but by a few "intellectuals."

The next few days were spent in Belgrade getting my bearings for the program in Serbia. This naturally began with an inspection of the Carnegie Library, which had just been completed and which, therefore, had very few books as yet on its shelves. As there was no free space for so large a building in the heart of the town where the old University stands, the Library had been built along one of the newer avenues leading to the suburbs and too

ARNEGIE LIBRARY, BELGRADE UNIVERSITY

far away for students who had classes in the old buildings. It was
explained, however, that all this would change with the rebuilding
of the University, for which plans were being drawn. Already
the new medical school had been built on the southern slope of
the hill, with aid from the Rockefeller Foundation, and its laboratories were stocked with instruments taken from Austria and
Germany on account of reparation. This was a kind of reparation
payment which I never saw anywhere else, and I could not imagine anything more appropriate. The result was to provide the
new medical school with the most up-to-date equipment, and, as
the professors had been trained in Vienna or Paris, the school itself was certainly in the position to open a new era in Balkan
medical history.

First of all, there was a formal visit to be paid to Mr. Nintchitch, the Minister of Foreign Affairs, on which occasion I was
accompanied by the Rector of the University. In this way the
unofficial character of my mission to the Balkans was underlined,
although, as will appear later, the government used to the full
every possible opportunity to be of help, and I was able to see
more than I had dared to hope of the country and people of
Yugoslavia during the short time I was there. Unfortunately, the
guiding genius of the country, Prime Minister Pashitch, was not
in Belgrade while I was there. One had a strange feeling, however, that he was never wholly absent from the minds of the
members of his cabinet, remaining always the dominating personality even when absent.

After the visit with Nintchitch, we went over to the American
Legation to call on our Minister, Mr. H. Percival Dodge. Owing
to the relatively informal nature of my plans, he had not been
informed of the purpose of my visit, which had never been com-
municated to Washington. He was most helpful, however, with
comments on Yugoslav politics and personalities, suggesting that
a little more officialdom would be useful in any country of Southeastern Europe. It was at his instance that the next day I took a
wreath to the tomb of the Unknown Soldier at the top of Mount

Avala, the last prong of the Rudnik Mountains, which the Serbian army held so long and gallantly against the Austrian invaders.

That evening I was surprised to find a large audience awaiting me at the Anglo-Yugoslav Club, where I had expected to find only a few club members. Avoiding politics, I made the talk wholly historical, describing the problems we had to face in preparing *The Economic and Social History of the World War*. Statistical estimates of the cost of the war were misleading, for there was no common standard of measurement. Money, and therefore everything else, had changed value so that merely stating the budgetary costs of governments did not give any accurate picture of the total displacement of the war. No history based merely on documents would tell the full story, although everything had to be checked against wartime records. This was beyond the capacity of individual historians for any one of the great powers. It had been calculated that it would take thirty-five miles of shelving to preserve the wartime output of documents of the British Government alone. Most of this documentation was not worth keeping, but it had to be sorted out.

In the absence of any statistics what was needed was a vivid description of the impact of the War and the suffering it had caused. It was hard for the imagination to grasp the full horror of the tragedy. If one could imagine a mobilization of the army of the dead, those killed in the war, it would stretch in ranks of four for about 3,000 kilometers, and would take about three years to pass a reviewing stand. And this did not include the still greater army of the wounded.

The Endowment did not believe, however, that merely recalling the tragedy, even in its most poignant aspects, would ever succeed in ridding the world of war. It proposed to study the cause as well as the effects of war, so that there would be something real for public opinion and for statesmen to fasten upon in the effort to find some other more civilized way for solving international disputes.

The Anglo-Yugoslav Club, although a thoroughly worthy

organization, was by its very nature somewhat suspect of political purposes, and that was an additional reason for not taking up there any questions of current politics. With the consent of the Rector, however, I widened the scope of the second address which I gave in the "gala hall" of the old University, making a plea for a structure of international peace as a substitute for the age-old resort to war as the instrument of policy. The substance of this lecture is a commonplace now, but that was hardly the case in Serbia in 1925. As a matter of fact it is, so far as I know, almost the first time that a war of aggression, which had been the controversial phrase in the debates at Geneva, was redefined in the old term of Clausewitz, "war as the instrument of policy." I had previously used this phrase in some public addresses in America and in an address before the Geneva Institute of International Affairs on my way to the Balkans. As the Belgrade lecture forms part of the record it is quoted in the Appendix.

It was especially important to awaken Serbian interests in the planning of their volume in the History, because I had already covered the story of the occupation of Serbia by the Austrian army in a volume in the Austro-Hungarian series, written by the Chief of Staff of the invaders, General Kerchnawe, and I made the point with some emphasis that we must not leave this as the sole record. As a matter of fact, General Kerchnawe's volume is one of the best documented in military history, describing the way in which a conquering army can turn conquest to the temporary advantage even of the conquered. For under the strict supervision of Kerchnawe's staff, the agricultural output of the occupied territory increased considerably toward the close of the War. This was established by statistics which Kerchnawe himself had transcribed with scrupulous care from the notebooks which he carried with him on his own person when, at the close of the war, the Austrian army was driven back in rout and most of the other records were lost. In spite of all this meticulous care of the Austrian soldier, his statements had to be checked over from the Serbian point of view. For this difficult task the Rector of the

University and several of the professors agreed that the most competent available scholar was Professor Dragolioub Yovanovich of the Department of Economics of Belgrade University. Professor Yovanovich was also highly recommended to me by both Professors Gide and Rist of my French editorial board, who had been his professors while he was a student at the University of Paris. Although still a young man he had already made his place in the University of Belgrade as one of its leading professors. A liberal in the truest sense of the word, his sturdy Serbian patriotism had been enriched and his outlook enlarged by his studies under such leaders of French thought as those who directed his education in Paris. No better choice could possibly be made for so delicate an analysis.

In view of the persecution which Professor Yovanovich suffered at the end of the Second World War, it seems not only fitting but necessary to carry the narrative forward at this point to give some idea of the volume which he wrote for the War History and also of his unwavering assertion of Serbian liberties against Tito's military despotism. The volume on *The Economic and Social Effects of the War in Serbia,* while based upon statistics wherever available, is a narrative of deep and wide human interest and sympathy. First of all, it begins with the story of the impact of the invasion—how the Serbian people fled before the invading troops and through the autumn and winter of 1914-15 crossed the mountains of Albania and Montenegro to seek safety in the Greek islands of the Adriatic. This chapter of European history, now almost entirely forgotten, stands out in the opening pages of the volume in a narrative based upon the author's own experience; it is so vivid that I quote a section of it in Appendix III. The English translation does not reproduce to the full the moving quality of the French, but this extract will give some idea of the masterly quality of the work as a whole.

It was perhaps inevitable that so strong an advocate of Serbian democratic freedom as Professor Yovanovich should fall victim to the tyranny of Tito. Never lacking in courage, he had persistently criticized some of the acts of Tito's government and was therefore tried for high treason. His reputation as a savant had, however, been so firmly established and his courage and integrity so well known in the learned world of Europe that protests at once were made from Paris and London; these may have had some effect in changing the court's charge of treason calling for the death sentence to imprisonment for nine years.

6 · Visit to Macedonia

AFTER A BUSY STAY of several days we left Belgrade for Macedonia as the guests of the government. We were supplied not only with a private car on the railway, but with motor cars at every step, an interpreter, and another young man from the Foreign Office, whose usefulness we never were able to divine and who submitted good-naturedly to constant teasing, and, above all, the Governor (Grand Supan) of the eastern part of Serbian Macedonia. Bishop Nicolai, with a young ecclesiastic as his assistant, was the unquestioned leader of our party as far as his episcopal seat at Ochrida.

After an easy run of a night and a forenoon, we stopped at the old capital of Serbia, Skoplje. Most of the names of places in Serbia were changed after the Turks were driven out, and therefore both geography and history are often puzzling. Skoplje was formerly Üsküb and was the capital city of the greatest and last of the medieval Serbian kings, Stephen Dushan, the remains of whose castle, built on the site of Roman and Turkish fortresses, still dominates the Vardar Valley. The monuments of the Turkish occupation are still visible in the dozen minarets whose narrow stems rise above the old mosques. Much more interesting, however, was the process of modernization of the city where the Turkish slums were being torn down and broad streets cut through. In the outskirts new houses were built, less in the European than in the American plan, with grounds around them. But no newly built American city would have an opera house as its first great public building. As at Belgrade, the Medical School of the University had been among the first to be restored, and a new Bacteriological (malaria) Institute had been erected on a grant from the Rockefeller Foundation. A large park was also being laid out. The whole development was so surprising that I questioned its financial soundness, for practically all of it had been built in the few years since the end of the World War. But I was told that the municipal authorities raised most of the funds locally and that it was not the unsound operation which one might suppose.

This instance of administrative capacity, which I later found matched at other places, seemed to me a sufficient answer to the skeptics in Vienna who doubted the ability of the Serbs, or for that matter of any Slav nation, to achieve anything worth while on their own account.

It is true that the cultural frontier between Germanic and Slavic Europe is clearly drawn and one of the most striking to be found anywhere. One notices it not only in the public buildings, shops, and homes of the cities, but in the houses of the farmers and in the roads themselves, where the paved road gives way to wagon tracks in sand or mud. But Serbia was already showing that the explanation for this lower grade of cultural life was to be found in the long history of exploitation of a people by no means devoid of native capacity. Proof of this lay at hand in Serbia, but on a much larger scale in the United States itself, where such miracles had been achieved by the immigrants from this part of the world.

We had been met on our arrival by civil and military authorities of the city and district, and after sightseeing in the city, were taken in autos (Buicks and Cadillacs) on an excursion through the countryside into a gorge in the mountains by the River Treska for a picnic lunch, where at the very road end is the tiniest of monasteries with a little chapel. The monks were gone, but the chapel still preserved its frescoes from the Middle Ages. I said this was at the road's end, but there were several places where the road seemed to end, as it wound along at some height above the river, with no parapet alongside. By a happy thought our meal was served country style, the great round loaf of bread, cooked in earthen kettles that had been heated in the coals of a small fire, was black and coarse but delicious. As we sat on the grass, baskets were brought us from the autos, and while the roughest, most ragged and soiled of the peasants sat in a group a little way off or helped to carry the food, we picnicked on Macedonian fare. The remains of the feast went to the villagers. Even when old and worn to rags, the peasant dress is picturesque: the little Eton jacket is trimmed either with brass or bits of bright-colored cloth; the trousers have a great decoration of black braid along the side stretched onto the brown homespun, and little embroidered slits here and there beside the braid reveal the linen underclothing.

The one thing which makes this picnic worth recalling, however, was an incident that happened on our way out, when we stopped to look at some recent excavations with Roman sarcophagi lying open on the roadside. Our Bishop, a marvel of quiet dignity, had gathered a group of a dozen peasants around him and for a while questioned and talked to them about their own affairs, comparing their life under Turkish rule with their present lot, and I suppose, as it was Sunday afternoon, there was a sermon thrown in. I shall never forget that scene, the Bishop in his long black robes and his tall round hat, carrying, as he nearly always did, his Bishop's staff, long and straight with stones set in silver at the end. An old man who must have been the Stareschina or patriarchal head of the community answered with the same dignity as the Bishop, and continued speaking for several minutes in a recital which evidently deeply affected the listeners, for everyone remained silent when he stopped. The reason for this was clear when the Bishop translated the talk, for the old man, pointing to the sarcophagi, had drawn a dramatic parallel with Serbian history. He said that his country also had remained buried for centuries and now at last had been brought out to "the light of freedom." This may have been Bishop Nicolai's own phrase, but there must have been something quite like it in the peasant's talk. It would be hard to imagine any more effective tribute to the liberation of the Serbian people.

Returning to Skoplje, there was no escaping the obligation to deliver another lecture in the hall of the University, which we found crowded with well-dressed citizens with a group of officers in the front row, all wearing their decorations. I took my text from the peasant's talk of the afternoon that the freedom Serbia had won would now have to be maintained by the upbuilding of the structure of peace, which could only happen under the regime of democracy. At the end Bishop Nicolai also spoke, summarizing the points I had made because, as he explained later, the translator had not done very well. There were some *givios*, and then we were driven to the hotel to be entertained at a formal dinner.

The next morning after breakfast we were ceremonially taken around the city, which we had not had time to examine on our arrival. Until the end of the World War the Serbs had only been in control of southern Serbia for the three years from 1912 to 1915. In the few years since then they had done wonders. It is a strange experience to pass in ten minutes from a modern, newly built city to the sections where the Turks are still sitting in their little shops, smoking or making things like silver ornaments, trinkets or shoes, or selling rugs. The bazaar in which these activities concentrate is much more picturesque than the modern section of the city. In the midst of it the old caravan center (caravanserai) stood out like the fortress it was when it was thronged by the traders of the East on their way to Budapest and Vienna. A huge double vaulted arcade is carried on heavy square columns around the courtyard, and the main building still shows almost no trace of the ravages of time.

Just on the edge of the city we drove past a gypsy town and saw a gypsy wedding. The bride was in a carriage with a bed sheet pinned carefully around so that no one could see her beauty, but she could not see anyone either. This seemed to be almost a touch of Turkish custom, recalling the way the Mostar and Sarajevo women would ostentatiously turn their backs on us and face the fields so as not to be seen, apparently not even trying to take a peek at us out of the corner of their veils. But then it should be said that the peasants generally affected a great indifference and seldom turned their heads to look at any of us. Curiosity is apparently something to be shunned in this part of the world.

After Skoplje the next stop was on a railroad siding at Gradsko in the Macedonian mountains where there was not even a station house. There were six motor cars, however, awaiting us, for the Supan here as everywhere else had everything planned in perfect order. No functionary from Austria or any other western country could have been more efficient. We motored for hours on a military road which I think has no parallel anywhere else in the world, for it is paved with white marble slabs. They said that it was much cheaper to use marble there than to bring commoner stones from a distance. The road lay through fairly open country like a white ribbon and showed no trace of the recent rains. By evening we had reached the provincial capital, Bitolj, which in our geographies bears its Greek name, Monastir. Here again I found that the Supan had forewarned the local dignitaries. A mass meeting had been called for eight o'clock, and it was already eight when our small caravan arrived at Monastir. We had had no dinner, and the Bishop insisted that we must eat, remarking that nobody ever was in a hurry in Serbia. So a very delicious meal was served, while a curious crowd stood patiently watching us eat. When the dessert was brought, they seemed to think that that was unnecessary and broke into loud applause at which everybody laughed good-naturedly. Then a great crowd turned out for the meeting, filling the largest hall in town to suffocation while I talked and the Bishop translated an address on the problems of war and peace. Again I felt sure from the frequent interruptions of applause that he had made it over into a sermon of his own. After the public meeting I met some of the leading citizens and particularly recall one of them, a leading doctor of the town, who had been educated in Paris and spoke perfect French. He told me that he was a Greek by birth and had been a Greek sympathizer in this disputed frontier area of western Macedonia, but he freely admitted that the government of the town and countryside had been much improved since Serbian occupation. He gave a graphic proof of this in describing his medical practice. He said that before the war he never risked going out by night in the streets of

Monastir without a guard and that at no time could he risk going outside the city to visit patients in the country or in adjacent villages. Now he said he went freely in both town and country without any guard and had never been molested because the Serbian rule guaranteed the peace. He went on to point out how much this meant to the country people when they were desperately ill or had had an accident. In the past there had been no way to bring them medical help. Now they had only to telephone into his office from the village post office and he could go at any time.

This evidence of good government by the Serbian authorities in Macedonia was backed up by others and later on I got from the Supan, who had accompanied us, part of the story of how the mountain feuds were being put down. The Serbian authorities had organized the Macedonians themselves in a volunteer security organization to suppress banditry and the *comitadji* who had been giving the country such a bad name. The volunteer police force had a loose military organization and wore an arm band in place of a uniform. It was something like the organization of the Vigilantes in our own Far West but with a slight touch of military pageantry supplied by the banners from different villages. I was sorry not to have seen their public meetings, some of which had taken place recently, but the Supan gave me pictures of them both in military formation and in the midst of crowds. He said that the population as a whole heartily appreciated the new regime of law and order and he thought that the old days of banditry in Macedonia were definitely over.

The next morning we were shown the town of Bitolj by the Mayor and the Governor of the district, taken through the market and the Turkish bazaar. Again there were the crowds of peasants, the women with embroidered white dresses and the men in coarse trousers and cotton coats decked with bright colors. There were donkeys and oxcarts and peasants carrying live chickens or baskets of red peppers, all combining to make a very gay scene. After looking at a Turkish mosque and the ruins of an old Venetian market of the fourteenth century which the city was planning to turn into a museum, we left for Ochrida. From Bitolj at the northern end of its mountain lake it was less than a day's motoring over the mountains to Bishop Nicolai's cathedral seat at the little town of Ochrida, at the head of the other somewhat smaller lake across whose waters lay the Greek frontier just over the horizon to the south.

Our arrival in Ochrida was different from anything else in our journey. When the people saw their Bishop returning they crowded around to welcome him and kiss his ring. Our progress through the streets was very slow, partly because the streets themselves are so narrow that at several places the car scraped the houses on both sides. But there was much scurrying down to the public square where the priests in their clerical robes were awaiting him, and when we stopped, there was a formal ceremony as though the Bishop had been away for a long time on a long journey.

Ochrida is a picturesque town clinging to a steep hillside. The second story of the old houses projects a foot or more to provide the balconies which, I suppose, were used in Turkish times as screened observation points by the Turkish women looking up and down the streets for the little items of gossip that might enliven their dull lives. There was a balcony like this on almost every well-built house, including the Bishop's palace, giving some shade to the hot cobblestone streets in summer time and some little protection against the autumn rains. As almost everywhere else in the Mediterranean, the roofs of the houses were built of heavy yellow tiles. Mohammedanism had apparently been pretty thoroughly rooted out here, because no minaret had been left such as we had seen at Monastir.

At the top of the hill was the little cathedral, eleven hundred years old, with heavy arches and walls covered with primitive mosaics. It was a rather squat, low-domed building, but in the churchyard beside it there was a newly erected tower, not very high but with an enormous bell at the top. This had been the gift of Professor Pupin, and the Bishop was very proud of it as its rich tones clanged out over the hillside and lake. There was no other bell in Macedonia to rival it. The church was in good repair, having been recently renovated. This explained, as I found out later, why the Bishop's palace was in ruins. The government had given him a fairly liberal subsidy to reconstruct the ramshackle old building in which he lived. Instead of spending the funds on his house, however, he had spent it all on the church, to the great dissatisfaction of the government, who did not like to have a high ecclesiastical dignitary living in quarters that were very little better than those of a slum, for the "palace," although it retained the outer dignity of an official residence, standing well above the neighboring houses and covering a large frontage, was in a state of utter ruin. In places the plaster had fallen from the ceiling and elsewhere hung perilously loose. Most of the timbers had half rotted away and the Bishop warned us not to go near the over-hanging floor of the balcony as it might give way into the street below. When a wind came up in the night it blew so strongly through the cracks in the floor that the carpet lifted from it, moving weirdly in the dark. The Bishop did not mind, because he was at heart a hermit as well as a mystic, but the King and Queen, who had been there in that royal progress which we saw culminate at Ragusa, must have wondered somewhat at the quarters assigned to them. We had the room where they had slept in two new brass beds, the only signs of opulence anywhere around. Fortunately the plaster did not fall on us while we were asleep and, in the company of the Bishop and his clergy, who were practically always at hand, we had a pleasant and instructive, if somewhat adventurous, visit to Ochrida.

In the evening the Mayor and the town councilors came to call. Two of them were Turks and they invited us to lunch at their house the next day. The Bishop said that in all his life in Macedonia he had never before known the Moslems to invite strangers to their homes. We could not accept, however, because the next morning we had to leave in order to keep our schedule. But the point that impressed us most was the friendly and neighborly way the Bishop and the Turks got on together.

In the morning the Bishop took us out on the lake for a ride in a new motorboat which the King had given the town on the occasion of his visit. The lake is absolutely shut in by hills, Serbian on the north, Albanian on the west, and Greek on the south. It is a very lovely mountain lake. After the boat ride was over the Bishop insisted that we call on the Mayor of the town because he was expecting us, but we found the real reason for the insistence when the Mayor, with great ceremony, presented me with a set of amber prayer beads which, I am sure, the Bishop had a hand in procuring. Then he gave us the inevitable Turkish coffee and we were allowed to depart with a ceremonial farewell to the Bishop and his clergy.

The Supan had been impatiently waiting for us to get started. We had had no breakfast as yet, only the after-dinner cup of coffee at the Bishop's palace and the Turkish coffee at the Mayor's. The plan was for us to have our breakfast at a fish station placed in the River Drina which drains the higher lake of Presba into the lake of Ochrida. There was a series of reed cages in the water in which the fish had been trapped. The Supan took a long-handled fork and began spearing the fish with great skill. He got three beautiful trout of about three or four pounds each, then took us along to show us how they would be cooked country style. In an upper room over a stable a man was crouching near the fireplace holding pieces of fish on a long spit. The priest who had accompanied us found the situation beyond his control and insisted that we should leave this primitive kitchen and go to the café for our meal. The Supan, however, looked at us in despair, for he had been counting on this country picnic and so, although it was raining, we decided to compromise and eat downstairs at the entrance of the shed. It was worth it, too, because the breakfast turned out to be all that the Supan had claimed for it—good bread and wonderful rosy trout and red wine, and the priest, somewhat reassured, enjoyed it as much as anyone.

We planned to motor back by another route, turning west to the nearby frontier of Albania and then north into the central region of Serbia, and could not understand it when we found that both the Bishop and the Supan were apparently putting every kind of obstacle in our way, insisting that the one comfortable journey back was the way we had come. However, we insisted upon carrying out our plan and, after a few days' stay, bidding the Bishop goodbye, with much reluctance at parting, we set off in our three car caravan. One of the cars was an army truck which was maneuvered so that we should not look into it and the Supan was always evasive when we asked questions about it. Later on in the day, however, on the edge of the Black Drina River, which our roadway followed closely, we ran into a mountain landslide, completely blocking the road with rocks, earth, and trees. There had been heavy rains the day before and this was not the only place in the roadway that was difficult. At once the mystery of the covered truck was solved, for out of it appeared four soldiers and an officer who set to work at once clearing the roadway. I had wondered why an army car had been provided, for when I looked inside the truck I found that they were heavily armed. There seemed no explanation and the Supan gave none, but two days later, when we reached Belgrade, we read in the newsapers that the day after we had passed along this road Albanian bandits had attacked the car in which the chief of Bishop Nicolai's clergy was riding, shot the chauffeur from ambush, and kidnaped two priests for ransom. Then I was told that it had been feared that word would get out in the mountain villages that a representative of a rich American foundation was passing along that roadway and that their plans were just one day out.

Our route ran along the side of the river between steep hills. To the west lay the frontier of Albania only a few miles back. Although it was evident that our escort was constantly on the alert we saw no one for many miles. Perhaps this is the time to insert a story which the Bishop had told us the night before we left. He said that two American women of the venturesome sort—he thought that they were college professors—had a few months before set out in spite of his protests to cross Albania without escort. They had just got well across the frontier when some fierce-looking mountaineers came up and confronted them in what seemed to be a threatening manner. German and French and Italian were tried on them with no effect, and then at last, English. The leader of the band suddenly changed his attitude, drew himself up and saluted with one word of greeting: "Wilson!" Identified as Americans, they were then treated with the utmost courtesy, but instead of being allowed to proceed across the mountains, they were gently led back to the Bishop's palace. I know of no other single incident which so graphically reveals the far reach of Woodrow Wilson's moral influence in the distant corners of Europe.

We left the Drina at Dibra (Debar) to strike inland across central Serbia, thus completing the circle from Skoplje. The rugged mountainous country was slowly left behind as we passed through cultivated lands to the towns of Gostivar and Tetovo, at both of which I found that official arrangements had been made to greet us on our arrival with the usual formalities and speeches. Happily, however, these could be cut short, for the day was wearing on and at Skoplje we had to catch the train back to Belgrade.

On arrival at Belgrade there were reporters waiting (also I imagine officially stimulated) for interviews on my impressions of Serbian Macedonia. Fortunately I was able to pay tribute to the indications I had seen on the spot of the way in which the old conditions of tribal isolation were being rapidly changed in the whole country. It was evident that the end of isolation was coming fast when we could go in a single afternoon from Skoplje to Monastir over a good motor road, whereas it used to take three or four days by mule track across the mountains. This opening up of the country was aided by the money sent in by immigrants from America—which, although not much in terms of national finance, was enough to give a new outlook to the life of many a backward village. But equally as important as these economic facts was the new political setup when government was no longer in the hands of corrupt Turkish officials working in close touch with Turkish feudal landlords whose one interest was to exploit the peasantry. The Serbian occupation had brought in a revolutionary change in the whole administrative system and in a few years had completely altered conditions of life. The arrangements for rural police which I described above were all the more effective because of the advantages of new and wider markets and better communications, and by the use of the telephone the police forces could be quickly mobilized even in distant mountain valleys. The result had been that perhaps for the first time in history the local volunteers were stronger at any given point than the invading *comitadji*. These practical methods of local statesmanship mean more in that part of the world than the discussions in Parliament or the making of laws that may never be applied.

In spite of these encouraging facts, agriculture was still primitive in the back country and there was much need of modern agricultural machinery to replace the primitive plows and harrows. Fortunately this was being done. At almost every railway siding one saw American farm machinery apparently bought through the Zadruga cooperatives. The need for reforestation was equally important to lessen the damage of erosion. The destruction of the forests by the Turks had dealt the country its worst blow, for on some of the mountainsides the soil was already so worn through that recovery would be costly, and the only way to save the land would be to plant forests on the mountainsides. There are, however, stretches of good soil still to be found in the open poljes, which have been carefully cultivated for centuries.

Above all, however, the chief asset of Serbia seemed to me to be the character of its people, a sturdy mountain stock, which throughout all the centuries of oppression had maintained a proud sense of personal freedom.

7 · Visit to Zagreb

BELGRADE looked good to us on our return from the gray skies and rains of Macedonia, for it was literally shining in the autumn sunlight. At noon Mr. Nintchitch, Minister of Foreign Affairs, gave us an official luncheon attended by about sixteen people, members of the Cabinet and university professors. This gave me a chance to explain more completely the work of the Endowment and the nature of the War History, taking advantage of the occasion to bring young Professor Yovanovich, as the one responsible for the Serbian volume, fully into the picture. The Government promised him every support in researches, a promise that was kept as the work progressed. Mr. Nintchitch told us that he had already arranged that we should leave for a visit to Zagreb and Croatia that evening, but I very much doubt if he knew that the Croatian leader, Stephen Raditch, whom I had met the year before in Geneva, had planned to go along with us. For as we talked with Raditch on the train it soon became evident that, as a very keen politician, he would be intent upon making political capital out of our visit and that I would have to be on my guard not to get drawn into the nationalist Croatian opposition to the Belgrade Government. But I had not counted on Raditch's energy, and although I spent only three days in Croatia he made the most of them.

Raditch was the absolute leader of the Croatian peasants, a demagogue of the first order. His methods seemed to me to be those of a Tammany politician multiplied many times over. For example, he claimed that he knew every Croatian by name and all their family histories. Unfortunately, as we motored through the countryside we came upon several of them who didn't know him, and he had to tell them who he was. Then they were properly impressed. In manner he was most effusive, to an extent rather offensive to one of the members of our party. And it must be admitted that he did not help matters by insisting on talking an unintelligible jargon which he thought was English. He was known as a strong supporter of the League of Nations and used it to good effect in the Parliament at Belgrade. But in his own home city it was clear to see that he was also using the leverage of his relations at Geneva to good effect as an influence for Croatian autonomy over against the ill-advised Serbian idea of a unitary state in which they could dominate. This was one place where provincial politics helped the movement for world peace.

But it would be unfair to Raditch and a wholly superficial judgment of his place in the history of Croatia if one failed to realize the solid basis of his political power. He was the creator of the Croatian peasant party; his whole life was attuned to the peasants' innate love of peace. The Croatian farmers had no such military tradition as that which the Serbs had cherished throughout the centuries. Raditch attacked Serbia's militarism as well as its political dominance and as a republican at heart was outspoken against the monarchy to a degree that sorely tried the strong but patient Pashitch. An idealist, Raditch held to the belief that there would not be wars if monarchies would give way to republics everywhere. This belief led at once to action, for soon after the formation of the Kingdom of the Serbs, Croats and Slovenes, Raditch proclaimed "the peacemaking republic" of the Croatian peasants in great mass meetings on the Zagreb fair grounds (the Sajmisti). Although his peasant followers were devout Christians, he substituted for the ideal of a universal Christian world as the promoter of perpetual peace an international movement of the peasants, which, renouncing war, would work only on the economic reconstruction of their countries. He dreamed of a new law of nations founded on a federation of these free peasant states and his vision made a deep impression on the Croatian country people. The meetings which he held on the Sajmisti had tremendous success, and for a time it almost seemed as if there were a real Swiss Landgemeinde and that the Peasant Republic was already founded.

But the administrative and political life proceeded on the old lines, almost entirely ignoring the idealistic beliefs held by the masses on the Sajmisti.

Few romances in the history of peace can match this episode in the life of the Croatian people and yet the outside world knew little about it and it is now buried in oblivion. Nevertheless, it explains the eagerness with which Raditch greeted the news from Geneva and America that there was an effort to outlaw war, for he saw in it the culmination of his own political ideas. The enthusiastic welcome which he gave me in Zagreb was unquestionably sincere.

The Belgrade Government had given us a guide to stay with us all the time, and we started sightseeing almost at once, visiting the very modern and splendidly equipped University Library, a monument of Hapsburg days. On our return to the hotel our guide was properly sidetracked, and from that time on we were in Raditch's efficient hands. An auto was waiting for us and as it was Sunday, which is their market day, we went at once to the city square where the market is held, and found it filled with peasants in their booths, practically all dressed in white cotton or linen, the women with short full skirts with brilliantly embroidered boleros edged or lined with white lambs' wool, white stockings and red garters, bright aprons and head shawls. Strangely enough, for once, the men's costume is prettier than the women's, as it has a better line. The white trousers are tucked into high black and polished boots. The blouse looks Russian, gathered in with a brightly colored belt and a very gay bolero of worked leather. Over this is worn a short, brown top jacket with orange or red braiding, sometimes draped picturesquely from one shoulder. It looked almost like a scene from an opera, only there was far too much of it for any stage. Here it was fitted into a strangely incongruous setting, for the large handsome square was surrounded by public buildings and shops, reminders of the fact that the Austrians had once been the rulers there, but the contrast between the monuments of bureaucracy and the folkways of the peasants

CROATIAN VILLAGE FESTIVAL NEAR ZAGREB

SCENE IN RUMANIA

BALKAN MUSICIANS

was a good indication of how the Hapsburgs had failed—or never tried—to reach down into the lives of the common people.

When the chauffeur saw that we liked the peasant costumes he suggested that we drive out to a festival at the village of Shestine which was not far away to see the country people in their native setting. We arrived just as Mass was over in the village church and everyone without exception was wearing the national costume. They seemed to like to have their pictures taken, and so a number of photographs were made, everyone in sight running to get into the group.

In the afternoon Mr. Raditch took us for a long drive into the country. He told us casually that the Mayor of the town had invited all the leading citizens to the city hall to hear me speak at five o'clock, but kept going along the country roads from village to village so that we were an hour late for the meeting. Giving the impression of not having planned it beforehand, he took us to the tomb of the Croatian poet, Preradovitch, where, in the presence of a group of villagers, flowers were handed us by peasant women to place on the grave of one whom Raditch regarded with evident reverence as his great predecessor. There were two more villages with similar "spontaneous" gatherings to which Raditch presented us, undoubtedly conveying the impression that this was an official visit from some member of the American Government.

The audience in the city hall had largely melted away, but a hundred or so still kept patiently waiting for our arrival. According to the account in next day's Zagreb paper I spoke for almost an hour in "very beautiful French," but then at the close, in spite of the lateness of the hour, Raditch translated the lecture, adding, I am sure, a good many points that were not in the original.

I do not remember anything of what I said on that occasion but hope that it was at least something like what the newspaper reported: that the time has come for a restatement of international law; that justice does not consist in merely emphasizing and defending our rights but in recognizing and accepting a decision which even if it appears to us unjust and harmful, is nevertheless necessary for the welfare of the whole body politic; that the problem of securing an enduring peace was the most difficult in all history and that it called for practical statesmanship as well as idealism. These are at least the main points in the newspaper report.

There was then a formal presentation of an album of the city of Zagreb and an artistically decorated medallion to commemorate the occasion. It was only later, however, that I understood why so much was made of the visit, for the year before Raditch had been one of the prime movers in Southeastern Europe in support of the Protocol of Geneva, having been misled into thinking that it represented the ideas of the United States because of the part which had been played by General Bliss, Mr. Miller, and myself at the Assembly in Geneva. Never doing things by halves, he had got together in Zagreb a great "national meeting" of something like 150,000 Croatian peasants to support the principles of the Protocol and by their support to strengthen his hand over against the Serbians in the national government. It was not until that evening that I learned how my name had been associated with this event, which helped to explain Raditch's interest in our visit.

The next day the Governor, the Ban, gave us a luncheon attended by representatives of the Church, military and civil authorities, at which, in addition to Mr. and Mrs. Raditch, I got to know Dr. Matchek, Raditch's lieutenant and successor. It was a very grand affair, again calling for speeches about the work of the Carnegie Endowment and the problems of peace. Then came visits to the former palace and the museum where we saw beautiful national costumes and embroideries, tea at the Raditches' home, and at last the day was over. The Foreign Office secretary found at the last moment that there was no *wagon-lit* on our train, and he held the train back until one was put on especially for us. I was to have made visits to other cities of Croatia but just before leaving I had received word from Bucharest that arrangements had been made there which prevented any further delay. The last day in Belgrade was a busy one with formal calls and a final reception at the Foreign Office in the afternoon, which was largely attended. From there we went directly to the night boat down the Danube for Rumania.

8 · Rumania and Its People

No OTHER COUNTRY in the world has a more magnificent gateway through its frontiers than that by which the Danube opens Rumania to the West. The Carpathian Mountains on the north are now entirely Rumanian, and the river slips sideways along their protecting bastions for over a hundred miles before it reaches the narrow defile. Then suddenly the sheer cliffs of the Kazan Pass rise up from the water's edge on either side from one to two thousand feet and the river narrows down from over a half mile in width to less than a thousand feet. So narrow is this cleft in the otherwise solid mountain wall that the wind as well as the water flows torrent-wise through it; even in calm weather there is always a miniature gale on the steamer's deck. There is nothing along the highlands of either Rhine or Hudson that can even distantly rival the impressive grandeur of this scene. The mountain pass, however, is not all. For just beyond it, where one might expect the lessening hills to grant free egress, the river itself becomes a barrier. Like a portcullis at the entrance to a castle, the jagged rocks of the Iron Gates protrude from the rapids of the pent-up stream. A dyked channel on the side at last flows into the quiet stretches of the lower Danube, and the road over the great plain of Wallachia lies free to Bucharest.

Only one people of the ancient world could force this formidable gate open to the march of armies. All along the southern wall of rock, at the height of a man's reach from the deck of a skiff, the regular succession of small square holes hewn in the precipice mark where the beams of engineers rested and were braced for the road that led from Dacia to Rome. The traces of this marvel of antique engineering reached all the way to Orsova, where the connecting roads across the hills to the north led to the heart of Transylvania. On the last of the southern cliffs, still decipherable from the steamer deck, one reads the inscription on a smooth-hewn entablature: IMP. CAESAR DIVI. NERVAE F. NERVA TRAIANUS AUG. GERM. PONT. MAXIMUS. Trajan's Column at Rome, with its spiral band of sculptured reliefs, still tells the story of the great exploit by which the frontiers of the Roman Empire were pushed to their farthest limit against that section of the barbarian north from which the tide of invasion was running strongest. Fortunately, this chronicle in stone is well preserved, with its gallery of over twenty thousand figures and its realistic pictures of Dacian dress and customs; for this record of the opening of the second century is the first and almost the only document on the ancient history of Rumania. Here, for instance, one sees the bridge across the Danube at Turnu-Severin—the Tower of Severus—with seven arches showing, of which only two or three fragments of piers are left, still monumental, rising from the quieter and wider stream.

But, however striking these visible memorials of the Roman past, they are certainly by no means so remarkable as the fact that the language of Rome was kept alive through all succeeding centuries, practically to the same extent as in Italy itself. And, some eighteen centuries after Trajan's conquest of Dacia, this nation bearing the name of Romans asserts not only its independence, but its right to be regarded as a cultural frontier of Western civilization. History has many examples of the hard endurance of sects or peoples under persecution, the most notable being the Jews; but no more remarkable instance of mere vitality and dogged persistence can anywhere be found than that furnished by this people, so long lost sight of by history itself. The villagers of the Transylvanian hills still wear the Dacian dress; their little houses are built like those that Trajan found there. The storms of ethnic invasion, of Goth, Hun, Magyar, and Slav, which swept away almost every vestige of the Roman occupation from the Danube Valley, never uprooted these poorest of peasants and shepherds. Perhaps their very poverty was their protection. But such an explanation only makes still more puzzling the fact that, illiterate and isolated, they still cherished in their impoverished inheritance the speech of ancient Rome, a distant western power, whose army was stationed north of the Danube less than a century.

This is not the place for a history of Rumania, but it is impossible to understand its present problems without some appreciation of its past. For Rumania has only in our own time emerged from what in Western Europe would be termed medieval conditions of life—or, in some respects, is still emerging from them. The process by which a nation acquires the elements of a new culture cannot be unduly hastened; it leaves uneven traces of the past, even when spurred by the attainment of political independence and the opportunities of a great future. In this regard, Rumania is like its neighbors to the south; for in both cases, the key to an understanding of their belated advance lies in the fact that, in the period when Western Europe passed through the so-called renaissance of art, literature, and science—from the fifteenth to the nineteenth centuries—the Turkish Empire stretched over all the eastern Danube region as well as over the Balkan lands to the south. The processes of the liberation of thought, of the development of political institutions, and the slow schooling in the rights and duties of citizenship which transformed the West were never shared by this people on anything like equal terms. If, therefore, there are anachronisms in its social or political structure which strike the Western visitor, if in its city life there are some regrettable imitations of the extravagances of so-called ultramodern ways, these matters of criticism are to be judged in a different setting than where the experiment of liberty is older. The peasant of the Wallachian and Moldavian farms is of as sturdy stock as that in the hills, and he is at last in a position to emancipate himself from the effects of that long oppression of Mohammedan Turk, mercenary Greek, or feudal rulers. The question for the present and future is whether and to what extent the responsibilities of government can be assumed by those so long its victims, and how they can mete out to others in their midst the justice so long denied themselves.

First of all, then, who are the Rumanians? The answer is by no means clear. The persistence of a Romance language must not be taken, as formerly done, as proof that those using it were also of Latin origin. There may have been a goodly number of "Roman" colonists during the second century of our era, but even if it were possible to imagine that the modern Rumanians are their descendants, this would not mean that they are of Latin stock in the strict sense of the word, for the depleted countryside of Italy proper furnished few such colonists in the distant provinces. There is evidence, however, which still further complicates the problem. For there are several hundred thousand "Rumanians" scattered through the Balkans, especially in Macedonia, and no one knows what their origins may have been. Their neighbors, especially the Slavic nations and the Greeks, have kept alive a name for them which indicates that they have always been a people apart, foreigners in the midst of another population. For the other name for Rumanian, the one commonly applied outside Rumania—at least until recently—is "Vlach," a variant of that Germanic word for the foreigner which made the Anglo-Saxons call their western neighbors "Welsh." Wallachia, the central plain which stretches from the Carpathians to the Danube, is, of course, "the country of the Vlachs." But this rich land was certainly not the uninterrupted possession (from Roman and Dacian days) of the Vlach, or the Rumanian, herdsmen and farmers. It was too much in the track of the storms of invaders from the eastern steppes. While the Rumanians were probably never dislodged from the Transylvania villages nestling against the northern slopes of the main Carpathian range—where they still dress as those did who served as models for the Roman sculptors of Trajan's Column—the chief cultural center of the Rumanian population during the Middle Ages was south of the Danube, especially on the Macedonian frontiers of Albania. How much the present Rumanians draw from the Balkan population would be hard to say, but all of this has but little bearing upon present problems, for, when modern history began, the Rumanian nation as we know it now was already established in Rumania. The dim chronicles of earlier days throw no real light upon the questions of today. What we find in Rumania is a singularly compact, distinctive nation, whose great achievement in the past had been its mere endurance, but which now, under the tutelage of its intellectual and political leaders, has become conscious of the cultural obligations which go with the maintenance of Latin speech. One feels the touch of the Middle Ages still in Rumania, but this people who survived the medieval anarchy did so less by an unbroken rigidity than by an adaptability to circumstance, which augured well in a new era when before them seemed to lie free fields of independence to exploit and no longer merely the narrow margins of oppression.

The Rumanian people are as unlike the Slavic peoples, who are their neighbors east, north, and south, as the Italians are unlike the Germans. And yet the great Slav movements which penetrated the Balkans in the Dark Ages must have passed through the very villages in which the ancestors of the present day Rumanians lived. This is so strange a historical fact that there have been many attempts to explain it; but none are satisfactory. The records of medieval history in that part of the world are so slight—the psychological evidences are slighter still—that it is doubtful whether the story will ever be sufficiently recovered to tell us how these simple peasants preserved a Roman speech and an ethnic consciousness in the midst of the moving forces of migration which swept over the countries at their side and incorporated the native stock into that of the conquering peoples.

There are little villages up in secluded valleys across the crest of the Carpathian Mountains which the ethnologist and the historian are inclined to regard as having persisted in the possession of Rumanian peasants from the old Roman and Dacian days. It may be so. In any case, these little hamlets of industrious peasants have more of a suggestion of romance, as romance is measured by the distance from the modern world, than perhaps any other similar settlements even in that romantic corner of the world. The high-thatched roofs and balconies along the sides of even the rudest and smallest huts, with lattice carved in the Roman arches, which are as perfectly proportioned as those the architects repeat in the new villas in Bucharest; the walls, bright red in autumn with the poles of ripening peppers, are quaint beyond description. The cattle and geese wander in and out from the meadows at the base of the hills; and on Sundays and on festival days, at church or on the village green, one sees the men come trooping along clad in the same sort of linen clothes that Trajan found among the Dacians and had his artists sculpture on the column at Rome before the Magyars had left the borders of Asia or the Slavs had moved from beyond the fenlands to the north. The women, too, dress with a quiet dignity in clothes less garish than one finds in many other peasant costumes, the fine linen of their kerchiefs chiefly enriched with gold needlework instead of color. Within these little houses the women year after year accumulate their store of linen folded away in boxes under the wooden seats all around the wall or piled above the framework of the great canopy bed. The floors are scrubbed with the cleanliness of a New England farmhouse, and every article is not only shining clean but hanging or set in its appointed place.

As long as these peasants maintain their ancient customs and live their lives uncorrupted by the influences of the great modern world, the Rumanian people will have an asset to draw upon similar to that which has made the strength of the great nations in the West.

But, however slight may be the original admixture of Latin blood, this does not prevent the Rumanians from being "Latin" in the same sense as the French, whose Gallic stock—of north European origin—so readily assimilated the culture of the Roman world. When one turns from Yugoslavia or Bulgaria to Wallachia, one is at once aware of a difference at least as marked as in crossing from Germany to France. The contrast with the surrounding Slavic world is not merely in the predominance of a different racial type (very much like the Italian in appearance, in ways of living, and in facile adoption of Western manners), but also in the architecture of their houses, with their ornamented roofs, their rounded porticoes and covered galleries, and in the boulevard life of their cities. Bucharest thinks of itself as another Paris. Yet, in both capital and countryside there are constant reminders of the common history of the Near East. Orthodox Byzantine churches bear witness to a common faith; and alongside the new and somewhat exotic angularity of Western streets, old-fashioned roadways wander haphazard here as they do in Yugoslavia, with similar little white houses behind the palings, presenting that indescribable quality of adaptation to circumstances which is the common mark of peoples who have lived under tyranny. This mixture of the old and new is rapidly changing and losing the impress of the past. But at present, combined as it is in an individuality all its own, it gives a peculiar charm to the people and country of Rumania.

The population of Rumania, however, is not all Rumanian, and in this lies its chief internal problem. Other ethnic islands have survived as well the floods of migration and the disasters of feudal and frontier warfare, and each of these by the mere fact of its continued existence has earned the right to some recognition within the framework of the modern state.

First of all, because highest in the scale of culture, there are the Germans of Transylvania. Although relatively too few in number ever to assume the character of a nation, these so-called "Saxons," whose history begins as far back as the eleventh and early twelfth century, have brought down into the distant plains on the fringe of eastern Hungary a Germanic culture as firmly established and as strongly built as the ancient castles of their seven cities—for the land of Siebenbürgen was a frontier post against the Eastern invader long before it withstood the shock of the Turk. Here where they treasure Goethe and Schiller in their schools, and Wagner and Strauss are symbols even more than they are at home, one comes at every turn upon the evidence of that century-long contact with the Germanic fatherland, politically so far remote. Such an element in the population, sturdy, enlightened, and industrious, does not fit altogether easily within the political framework of a state in which it forms a relatively small minority; but given the chance for economic development with due regard to its strong feeling for its cultural heritage, it is an element which may add greatly to the strength of the nation of which it forms a part. Long held under the sovereignty of Hungary, Transylvania, in its adjustment to the new conditions after the war, would naturally present some difficulties, but in the Germanic element in these lands west of the Carpathians there is an added capital stock in intelligence and industry much greater than the material resources. The trade that once flowed through the Carpathian passes and enriched these border cities should once more revive the all but forgotten history of the merchants who opened this mountain gateway of the East. In the old Lutheran church of Brasov hangs what is perhaps the greatest single collection of ancient oriental rugs, the gift of Brasov merchants returning with their caravans from the Orient. This historical witness to the activity of the medieval and modern trader may well be paralleled again by a revival of the old-time overland commerce with Eastern markets, by train and auto; but there is no denying that in order to accomplish this the problems of Transylvania will have to receive a treatment at once statesmanlike and far-seeing, with an eye to the interests not merely of the old Rumania on the one hand nor of Transylvania on the other, but to the stimulation of trade and industry throughout the whole Near East. The prosperity of Transylvania depends, in the last analysis, upon the entire situation in Southeastern Europe.

Unfortunately, however, the problems in this part of the world are less economic than political or racial, using that word in the loose sense of national differences. The persistence in Siebenbürgen of the unabsorbed Germanic element shows how strong are the ties of blood and common culture. But by far the strongest nationalism was that of the Magyars, who, having lorded it over the whole central plain of the Danube and the Transylvanian uplands for a thousand years—except when temporarily conquered

by the Turks—were in no mood either to surrender to Rumanian
sovereignty or to accommodate themselves to it. The still more
venerable claims of the Rumanians or Vlachs went back beyond
the age of the barbarian invasions to ancient Dacia, but never,
until the twentieth century, had there been any serious effort to
translate this lost historical force into politics. Rumanian nationalism was, even more than that of Serbia or Bulgaria, the result of
the decline of Turkish power, for the two principalities of Wallachia and Moldavia, out of which it was formed in 1858, had no
such history behind them as that of Stephen Dushan. Therefore
the Rumanian intellectuals began an artificial movement to gal-
vanize the latent sense of national feeling which every people
cherishes more or less. The efforts of Count Apponyi to Mag-
yarize the minorities of Hungary and of Prussia and Germanize
the Poles inside its eastern border were copied and applied from
Bucharest. The result was to create antagonisms among neighbors
who in all the long past had managed to get along with each other.
Naturally, the clash was greatest in Transylvania, and when, in
1920, as a result of the World War, the Magyars had to yield their
age-long sovereignty to the Rumanians, it was beyond human
nature for the new situation to be accepted with good grace. The
Magyar slogan in defiance to the Treaty of Trianon, their counterpart to the Versailles treaty, was "No, no, never" (*"Nem, nem,
soha!"*), painted on almost every signpost or public building from
Pressburg on the west of the new frontier to Szegedin on the east.

Left to themselves, the so-called better classes in Central and
Eastern Europe were sowing the dragon's teeth of future wars.
The only way to meet and counter their stimulation of animosities
was that of the League of Nations, a fact well recognized and
honestly acknowledged at that time. For no one ever paid more
eloquent tribute to the League than this same Count Apponyi,
who was willing to work side by side with his Rumanian and
Czech colleagues, in spite of the inadequacy of the Minority Commission. But the poison of nationalism was working too strongly
in the body politic of Europe for any rapid cure by appeals to

reason, and, before the slow process of education could work, Fascist and Nazi appeals to force and violence won the day.

Apart from the Bulgarian question in the Dobruja south of the Danube, the other population problem of Rumania, and the one concerning which we hear most, is that of the Jew. There are great numbers of Jews, especially in the eastern sections of Rumania. The problem which they present to the government is not an easy one for, largely through the fault of the Christian population, and also largely through their own fault, they have been too little assimilated not only in the social life of Rumania but also even in its economic life. It should be said that this condition exists more or less throughout all Eastern Europe and perhaps more especially in Poland. And yet the Jewish question is not merely one of social and political adjustment. The Jewish population of Rumania has contributed culturally, economically, and even politically to the sum total of European civilization even far beyond what one might expect if one sees the conditions of the depressed masses. Some of the keenest thinkers in Europe today are Rumanian Jews.

It would be a mistake, however, to allow the problem of minorities so to overshadow the Rumanian scene as to obscure the interests of the Rumanians themselves, for even in the greater Rumania of the postwar days they preponderate by far; and in dealing with them one should not be misled by the superficial appearances of the capital, Bucharest. Bucharest is no more typical of the Rumanian peasant than Paris is of the French peasant. In both cases, there is a sturdy stock hardened by privation in the past, intent upon the simple routine of its farming and village life, gay, and yet not dissolute. Having now broken down the last remnants of feudal privilege by dividing up the great estates, the Rumanian peasantry has entered, in the opening of the twentieth century, into the same general economic situation as was won by peasants of France and North Germany a century or so earlier. There is much to hope for and relatively little to fear from the sober commonsense of these hardworking owners of the soil, worthy successors of the ancient Dacians.

So far I have been speaking only of the population, but the homeland of these people is as varied as the inhabitants. Mountain and plain, marshland and forest, the open steppes and the rugged Carpathians—each contributes its appropriate produce to the economic resources of the country. So comprehensive are these resources that, potentially and in their variety at least, they are probably rivaled by no other country of Europe and perhaps by no other civilized land, outside the United States. It has been claimed that Rumania can produce practically everything except rubber and cotton. Its wheat supply was perhaps the greatest single prize gained by the Central Powers during the World War. The products of the soil are singularly like those of the United States, due to a similarity of climate between the two countries, a similarity not shared by Western Europe. Corn and fruit ripen as in the Mississippi Valley and the fertility of the soil was never exhausted by the relatively simple agricultural methods of the past.

Of its mineral wealth, the chief, as well as the most distinctive, is petroleum. The plains around Campina are as thickly spiked with the oil-well derricks as the busiest sections of our own oil country. The coal mines of Rumania are less known outside its frontiers, though the output totals about three million tons. Less striking but more picturesque are the great salt mines; while in the mountains of Transylvania, the peasants still wash down from the hillsides the gold which was a notable product of ancient Dacia. Handmade water wheels by the roadside pound the pebbly quartz, while the peasants work on the fields alongside. But most of the mineral wealth of the Carpathians still awaits the modern engineer. Only recently have they begun to work the quarries which produce quicksilver, and a similar introduction of modern methods would be amply rewarded from the at present hidden sources of supply.

The economic resources of Rumania hold the promises of a prosperous future. But no such promises can be realized either here or elsewhere without regard to the difficult questions of policy and of administration. In this respect, the current economic history of Rumania resembles that of its ethnic and social elements. The development of resources will depend as much upon the development of markets as upon the machinery of production. Broad policies of accommodation with other nations are therefore implied, but the peace treaties, by creating a Greater Rumania at the cost of its three neighbors, Hungary, Bulgaria, and Russia, made any plans for economic cooperation with them extremely difficult. It was clear to some of us at the Paris Peace Conference that the political settlement which gave Rumania so much, more than double its previous size, could not be a permanent settlement, or if it were, would always be a provocation to a future war. Hungary had sworn that it would not rest until it took back Transylvania and pushed the frontier of Rumania once more back to the crest of the Carpathian Mountains. Bulgaria regarded Dobruja as its richest agricultural province and Soviet Russia would scheme and plan against Rumania until it recovered Bessarabia. The idea of Rumanian nationalism, however, was running high in 1925 and there seemed to be no way to check it.

But we must now turn to the narrative of the journey which began at Turnu-Severin where our boat arrived about three in the afternoon. The train for Bucharest, however, had left an hour before, and we were obliged to wait there overnight, when the next train came through from Sofia to Bucharest, arriving at seven o'clock in the morning. I had arranged to have Mr. Mitrany come down from London to meet us and travel at least part of the way with us through his native Rumania. I have already spoken of his contributions to the history and politics of the Near East and especially of Rumania itself. He was not only a delightful companion but a sound advisor in the arrangements of the Rumanian volumes of the War History.

After having been comfortably established in the best hotel, which like most of Bucharest was a definite imitation of Paris, I went to pay my respects to M. Duca, the Foreign Minister who at Geneva had so cordially extended the invitation to visit Rumania.

Cordiality of the official kind is not always genuine, but on this occasion it proved to be so, for M. Duca at once arranged meetings with the Prime Minister, John Bratianu, and Vintila Bratianu, his brother, the Minister of Finance, who were the leaders of the Liberal Party and the two most powerful figures in the recent history of Rumania. Their father had been the king-maker who secured the election of Carol I to the throne of Rumania in 1866, and independence from Turkey in 1877. His son John, who had been Premier during the War, had attended the Paris Peace Conference where I had met him, although only casually. In 1925 he was the virtual dictator of the country. It was with the younger brother, however, with whom I had to deal in planning the Rumanian volumes of the War History and he proved to be most helpful, although he did not disguise his disappointment that we were omitting from the narrative the political history of the war, in which he was chiefly interested. Neither Mr. Mitrany nor I was entirely satisfied with the conservative auspices under which the Rumanian history was launched, but he agreed with me that it was the only way to secure full cooperation, for the government kept a close hand on all university activities. Once satisfied that we would not take sides politically, the government was most helpful at every stage of the work.

I felt, however, that I would appear to be drawn into Rumanian politics unless I also met the leader of the opposition Peasant Party, M. Maniu, who proved to be a most intelligent and generous-minded politician. He understood my position perfectly and heartily approved of the way in which we were setting about securing Rumanian collaborators for the History. Preliminary negotiations were entered into at once, especially with Professor Antipa, but final plans were left until my return from a journey to Transylvania, for it was part of the plan of M. Duca that we should leave Bucharest as soon as possible to visit the King and Queen at their summer residence at Sinaia in the foothills of the Carpathians and go on from there over the mountains of Transylvania.

The route north from Bucharest is level open country, but in spite of the fact that it seemed like good farming land the houses of the peasants were poor beyond description, mere huts, distinctly inferior to those of the Yugoslav peasantry. About half-way to Sinaia we passed through the great oil region of Ploesti, with its forest of derricks and the black seepage from oil tanks. From there it was by no means a royal road that led to the summer residence of the royal family, although the Ploesti oil wells are, next to agriculture, the greatest economic resource of the country. From the station at Sinaia we motored down along tree-lined avenues to the castle.

The castle itself is definitely built in the German manner, apparently under the influence of the uncle of King Ferdinand, King Carol, who came from the younger branch of the Hohenzollern family. The architecture is of that somewhat fussy unrestful type which one sees here and there in south Germany, with ornamental timbering in stucco walls with contrasting stretches of red brick or stone and surmounted by sharp belfry-like roofs. All in all, it was not a restful spot, even when seen from the long Carmen Sylva Avenue. But inside it was homelike and unpretentious, the whole atmosphere quite restful. We were accompanied from Bucharest by a Foreign Office official who seemed somewhat disturbed by the fact that I did not wear striped trousers and a morning coat, as prescribed by protocol on all such occasions. M. Duca, however, who went along with us, reassured me that both King and Queen ran their court with informality, and that proved to be the case. As we went in, we were received by the King's aide de camp and the Queen's lady in waiting, who showed us our seats at table, a little removed from the center. The Queen wore a beautiful costume with a white embroidered waist and headdress and a red skirt. The King was quietly dressed in a dark business suit. Their two daughters, the Queens of Yugoslavia and Greece, were visiting them at the time. When we got to the table, Queen Marie said, "Mr. Shotwell is to sit beside me and Mrs. Shotwell over there, beside the Queen of Yugoslavia."

The lady in waiting was disturbed and said to Mrs. Shotwell, as she rearranged things, "There the Queen goes again upsetting all the arrangements, as usual." However, the change had to be made and everyone talked very animatedly, mostly to us.

The Queen of Greece was the quietest member of the family group. She is a very beautiful woman with red hair, and is inclined to be stout. The garrulous lady in waiting attributed it to eating candies! The Queen of Yugoslavia was much interested in our trip through Serbia and talked very pleasantly about it. She was much amused about the state of the Bishop's palace in Ochrida and that hanging ceiling in the bedroom where we had slept.

King Ferdinand, sitting across the center of the long table, opposite Queen Marie, at first took little part in the conversation going on around him. He seemed a little out of it, and acted as if he didn't care. But when Marie told him, with an obvious attempt at casualness, that she had invited a prominent leader of the international movement for woman's rights to have tea with them, he reacted without reserve, and she had to reassure him at length that he would not be backing a radical feminist. He held stubbornly to his point, and we were only saved from embarrassment by Marie's retreat from the proposal. The tea would be with her, but she hoped he would turn up! After this little incident such as might happen at any family table, the King grew more animated, but never quite equaled the vivacity of his irrepressible wife.

After the luncheon was over the King took me off into a corner of the sitting room and kept me there for about an hour while the Foreign Office official, much upset, walked ostentatiously by from time to time as though to relieve the King and give him a chance to escape. However, before the hour was over, he sent the diplomat away and we continued our intimate talk. There is nothing, however, to report on this except for the fact that it was a talk with royalty and that the King seemed happy to have a chance to talk about American politics, especially about Woodrow Wilson and his struggle with the Senate. I had heard critics of the King speak slightingly of him, but I left Sinaia filled with admiration for the deft way he held the conversation off the problems of Eastern Europe and yet never gave the impression of consciously doing so. The nearest we came to the subject was in discussing the Paris Peace Conference in academic terms. His bearing was modest and without a trace of formal ceremony.

In the late afternoon we started north up a Carpathian pass along which there were constant traces of the trenches held by the Rumanian army in 1916, for we were passing through one of the great battlefields of the war. The invading army, drawn not only from Hungary and Austria but from Germany as well and under German leadership, began its advance through Transylvania and down the Danube Valley with the speed and confidence of a victor. But that was while the Rumanian army was officered by the dandies from Bucharest, the kind of officers who, rouged, white-gloved and mincing, could play their part in a salon but not on a battlefield. After they had disappeared in the first rout of the Rumanian army, the peasants themselves dug in along this mountain crest and held their line so well that the Germans were never able to drive through them. This, at least, is the story I was told on the spot. There were undoubtedly strategic reasons for the concentration of Mackensen's forces in the more open country to the south instead of in the mountains. But in the Rumanian account the credit for holding the line was due entirely to the morale of the peasant soldiers.

This story reminds me of one other that shows an equal courage and steadfastness of the common man, in contrast with the effeminacy and cowardice of the socialites who had got their military commissions by favoritism. Everyone knows that the Portuguese troops broke and fled from their sector which was held alongside the Canadians on the Western Front, but it is not recorded in history that later on, after the officers had been displaced, the Portuguese peasants came back to the front line under Canadian leadership and held under the heaviest barrages. The story can best be pointed up perhaps by recalling that when the Portuguese army paraded before the Belgian King Albert on the sand dunes near Boulogne, a rain storm came up and the officers marching at the head of their companies put up umbrellas, to the scorn of all seasoned soldiers. Detractors of democracy may well consider these exploits of the Rumanian and the Portuguese peasantry.

These memories of the World War were soon forgotten as we came into the old trading city at the northern end of the pass, called by the Rumanians Brasov, but under the Hungarians retaining its German name of Kronstadt. The population of the city is still largely German belonging to that colony of Germans which was planted during the twelfth and thirteenth centuries to hold the Carpathian frontier against invasion from the east. Throughout all the centuries these Germans, locally known as Saxons, have retained their Germanic culture with almost fanatic zeal. We had a good illustration of this the evening we arrived when we went with the Rumanian officials to the opera house to hear a Strauss opera. Between the acts when, as in all European opera houses, the audience promenades in the foyer we had the strange sensation of feeling like ghosts, for the Saxon burghers made it perfectly clear that anyone coming under the auspices of the Rumanian government was totally unwelcome. There was no incivility, but everyone acted as though they did not see us, not with averted eyes but looking straight through us to the wall behind. It was a mass demonstration of solidarity and innate racial hostility and arrogance.

The town is now the chief manufacturing city of Transylvania and still keeps up an important commerce with the East, and with typical conservatism the money changers are still to be found at small tables in the streets and market place. Nowhere else is there a better example of the way in which the peoples along the eastern frontiers of Europe have lived as neighbors for centuries without losing their mother tongue or their sense of nationality. Although the Germans, Magyars, and Rumanians meet together in the inner town, they still wear their distinctive national costumes, bargain with each other in broken idiom, and continue to live in separate suburbs as they have done in the past.

This situation was even more apparent in Sibiu (*German*, Hermannstadt; *Hungarian*, Nagyszeben), still the seat both of the Greek Orthodox (Rumanian) Archbishop and of the head of the Protestant churches of Transylvania. The town was founded by a certain Hermann of Nuremberg about the middle of the twelfth century and, like Brasov, grew rich as a station on the trade route with the East. All its public buildings were in the German style. I was surprised to find that the art gallery and library had not been in use, at least in recent years. However, from the great care that was taken of both pictures and books, one could see the continued pride of the German population in what to them were the treasures of Western culture. A greater surprise, however, was awaiting us an hour or so later when we were driven out to the village of Selistea in the mountains, which the Prefect told us had preserved absolutely untouched by any outside influence the customs, as well as the costumes, of the ancient Dacians. It was an amazing experience to see these figures of history come to life, as it were, moving in and out of the lovely old peasant houses, scattered somewhat unevenly along the village street. They were all in their best clothes because there were two village weddings that afternoon, and we stayed on with the Subprefect of the town who encouraged the villagers to continue singing and dancing for us. It was as if all the centuries of European history had suddenly vanished and we were back in the days of Trajan.

From Sibiu we went by train to the university town of Transylvania now called Cluj (*German*, Klausenburg; *Magyar*, Kolozsvar). Here, as in Zagreb, we were suddenly brought back to the nineteenth and twentieth centuries. The University which was only founded in 1872 has magnificent up-to-date buildings and the university quarter is surrounded by many mansions built by the Transylvanian nobles as winter homes. We had no time for sightseeing, however, because we were met at the station by the Minister of Fine Arts, the Prefect, the Mayor, and other local dignitaries. The students from the upper schools were lined up at the entrance of the station, the girls in national costume and the boys in Boy Scout uniform. At noon there was a grand banquet and in the afternoon I talked (in French) to an audience packed like sardines in the Aula of the University where, to make matters worse, ventilation was entirely lacking. Although almost the entire faculty of the University had turned out for the occasion, I sensed again, as at Brasov, an underlying hostility to the Rumanian Government. The Magyars, however, are subtler than the Germans and partly disguised their feelings by outward politeness. Conscious of the delicacy of the situation I avoided present-day issues by stressing the movement for international peace back through the centuries, with the culmination in the declaration in the Protocol of Geneva that aggressive war is a crime. I had a distinct feeling, however, that even this purely academic treatment did not register.

The next day we were driven by motor about 160 miles through the mountains to Alba Iulia, the place of the coronation of the King. In the heart of the Carpathians there are magnificent birch and pine forests, but the roads were terrible. At times the mud went over the hubs of the car wheels; the auto would skid to within a few inches of the unprotected edge of the precipice. The Prefect reassured us by saying that his car had turned over three times with him and he had never been injured. I came to the conclusion that the chauffeur was really testing our nerves on purpose.

One of the most interesting sights along the roadway on this journey was the row of ordinary-looking dwelling houses with a small stream sluiced alongside each one so as to turn a little water wheel with rapidly turning hammers fastened to the axles; the hammers pounded little piles of quartz in the running stream to release small bits of gold ore, which were then panned in the manner of California placer miners. It was the most primitive industry I have ever seen and yet not the least ingenious. Wholly different and ultramodern was the machinery at the oil fields, where we paused while the engineers explained the various processes of refining.

Then, about a week after we had left it, we were back in Bucharest, where I found three tasks awaiting me before our departure: first, the delivery of public lectures at the University; second, the completion of plans for the Rumanian volumes in the War History; and third, the round of official meetings and entertainments. I should have been glad to escape from the lectures, for the rigors of the Carpathian journey in November weather had brought on a severe case of grippe. But it was too late to back out and so we went ahead with the arrangements for two lectures, one at the Rumanian Academy and the other at the Rumanian Social Institute. The audience at the Rumanian Academy was largely drawn from university circles and my lecture dealt with the history of war from ancient times to the present, ending with a description of the Carnegie Endowment efforts to make a scientific study of the nature of war today. The second lecture was a more important public occasion and was attended by the Prime Minister and almost his whole Cabinet. Professor Gusti, the President of the Institute, has a European reputation as a social scientist of the first order, and his strong endorsement of the lecture was duly noted in the Bucharest papers. It was an ordeal for me, however, because on the evening of the lecture I was running a temperature somewhere in the neighborhood of 103 and had neither time nor strength to prepare written text, so I was obliged to speak *ex tempore*. Nevertheless, the combination of circumstances proved favorable; when, a few days later, I read over the stenographic account of what I was alleged to have said, it needed almost no corrections before printing in both the original French and later in an English translation (finally published in April, 1927, in the Endowment's International Conciliation Pamphlet Series under the title "A Turning Point in History"). Because this lecture dealt in greater detail with the theory of the polity of peace which I had touched upon in the Belgrade address, it also is reproduced in the Appendix as a further step in the development of the idea which two years later was to be incorporated in the Briand-Kellogg Pact.

In the planning of the War History volumes I had the invaluable help of Mr. Mitrany, who later contributed the volume on the land reforms of Rumania and the general volume on the effect of the War in Southeastern Europe—two masterly and scholarly volumes. But there was a delicate problem to be solved because the outstanding authority in Rumania, Professor Iorga, would normally be chosen for this task. Although primarily a political historian, Iorga had done more than anyone else to recover the elusive traces of Rumanian social history from the Roman period through the Middle Ages which, owing to the recurring invasions, were dark ages in that part of Europe down to modern times. A member of the learned academies of Europe and an honorary president of the World Conference of Historians, Professor Iorga would have given distinction to the Rumanian series but, a man of untiring energy, he had not rested content with research and had been taking an increasing part in politics. As great care had been taken in the planning of the War History to avoid political controversy, it was therefore necessary to choose a substitute from among those members of the University who had played an important part in the economic mobilization of the country during the war and in the subsequent measures of postwar adjustment. This pointed definitely to the choice of Professor Antipa, who had held important posts in the wartime government and, as a statistician, had special advantages in access to secret wartime documents.

There were more elaborate plans but they are of no interest now because, apart from Mr. Mitrany's studies, the only Rumanian contribution to the War History was Professor Antipa's study of military occupation and its effect upon the Rumanian people. There is no record, like the Serbian volume, of the human tragedy which the War brought to this part of Europe.

In this part of the world formal calls on dignitaries, receptions, and dinners are more than social obligations—they come at the beginning and the end of every important piece of work. By coincidence we were able to watch the procession of prelates, soldiers, and statesmen installing a new patriarch of the Orthodox Church and afterwards were given a formal introduction to the Patriarch, meeting twelve of his bishops at the same time. Having Bishop Nicolai in mind I talked Peace to one and all, but I had the distinct feeling that there was less of other-worldliness and much more of politics in this clerical group than in Yugoslavia. In spite of the colorful display, the incident really amounted to very little.

Quite different, however, was the final dinner which we gave to Prime Minister Bratianu, M. Duca, and other members of the Cabinet. It was attended as well by our Minister, Mr. Culbertson, whom we had known in Geneva and who had been extremely helpful throughout our visit. He had in the course of the afternoon drawn together a distinguished company of Rumanians to meet with members of the American colony in order to establish a permanent American Rumanian organization in Bucharest.

The next morning we left by train for Bulgaria, the government placing an official car at our disposal.

9 · Bulgaria

WE CROSSED the Danube at Ruschuk and found that the Bulgarian Government had sent down another special carriage for the night journey to Sofia, with a Foreign Office official in charge who had been specially trained for this kind of service and who bore the weirdly appropriate—or inappropriate—name of Kissimoff. He was an experienced diplomat and throughout our stay in Sofia was most solicitous and helpful. Perhaps I should add here that in none of the countries we traveled through had there been any request made for official railway carriages or any other privileges of travel.

It was late afternoon when we left Ruschuk, but still daylight as we turned away from the river and began to mount slowly into the hills. These were forest-clad like those of Bosnia, but there were glades opening into the valleys where villages nestled comfortably in the midst of small fields. These are foothills of the Balkan ridge of mountains that runs from the Black Sea over toward Serbia; we saw little of them, for night soon settled down.

We arrived in Sofia on a gray November morning. My time schedule was now beginning to press upon me, and I could allow myself only three days in Bulgaria. This meant concentrating entirely on Sofia. Fortunately I had arrangements beforehand which helped me to deal at once with the preparation for the Bulgarian volume of the War History which was entrusted to Professor Georges T. Danaïllow, an economist of European reputation, and what was most important and most difficult to find in this part of the world, an economist who was not a political propagandist.

Sofia makes upon the American visitor an impression different from that of Belgrade or Bucharest. It is more genuinely modern, having been almost entirely rebuilt since the 1890's. The streets are well paved and clean and the buildings are without false ornamentation. This is significant, for architecture is a kind of unconscious language which nations use—a language determined not only by the conditions of wealth or poverty, but by the temper and outlook of the people, as well. Almost every description of the Bulgarian people pays tribute to their sincerity and integrity. This is certainly the characteristic note of the city of Sofia. It lacks the suggestion of gaiety of old Vienna or the pretensions of Belgrade, or the ostentatious display of Bucharest. It is dignified and self-respecting, and almost wholly western in aspect.

There was, however, a grim reminder in the cathedral in the center of the town that all was not well in Bulgaria, for the debris of that domed structure still lay thick in piles along the sides of the walls from a giant bomb which had been exploded six months before (April 16), during the funeral of a general who had been murdered the previous day. The cathedral itself was an ugly modern imitation of Byzantine art, massive and heavy, with striped walls, almost like prison clothes—one of the least imaginative of all the public buildings I have seen. The explosion had killed over a hundred people and wounded over a hundred more. Martial law had been proclaimed and the police had arrested some five thousand persons throughout the country, employing methods of suppression of the ruthless type familiar in the past to that part of the world. Although no general uprising had followed, the situation was still tense in November, much more tense than I knew at the time.

As a matter of fact, Bulgaria, which at the turn of the century was outstripping its neighbors both economically and politically, and as such had become the favored Balkan country in both England and the United States, had, from the very beginning of its independence in 1908, suffered a series of setbacks which led to almost constant strife. The chief architect of its calamities was Prince, later King, Ferdinand. This "wily fox" was a German princeling who, by intrigue and the skillful use of the anarchy resulting from the breakup of the Turkish Empire, managed to transform the Bulgarian principality into a kingdom, but who, by his pro-German ties and autocratic tendencies, ran counter to the newly awakened nationalism of the Bulgar peasants. Their champion was Stambulisky, one of the greatest figures in all Balkan history, typically Bulgarian in his obstinate defense of peasant rights, a rough-hewn character who dared even to threaten the King, when Ferdinand proposed joining the Central Powers in the World War. The result was a sentence of life imprisonment, from which he was freed in 1918 to negotiate at Paris what could be saved for Bulgaria after it had been defeated and surrounded by victorious enemies. In spite of his successes abroad, however, Stambulisky's social and economic program at home was carried out by an organization of the peasantry which roused the opposition of intellectuals, townspeople, and officers of the army, who joined together for his overthrow and murder by a *coup d'état* in the summer of 1923. At least two of his reforms, however, were destined to be widely copied: the land laws limiting the size of farms, and the drafting of the youth into peacetime labor battalions, a device which lasted on and was later adopted by the Nazi as an invention of Hitler.

This slight sketch fails utterly to convey the sense of the greatness of Stambulisky in the eyes of his contemporaries, especially of his peasant followers. Years later, in 1940, his secretary of those days, Theodore Geshkoff, studied with me at Columbia University and under my direction wrote a volume called *Balkan Union*, which is both dedicated to the memory of Stambulisky and bears the mark of that enduring loyalty to a lost leader which is one of the finest qualities in anyone. But, even then, Dr. Geshkoff was constantly aware of the continuing vindictiveness of Stambulisky's enemies. It was, therefore, a foregone conclusion that acts of violence like that of the murder of the General and the bombing of the cathedral were regarded as reprisals.

But there was another element in the situation which touched my own interests more nearly. For the question of Macedonia was also involved. In his great plans for an ultimate Balkan union, Stambulisky had not only carried out loyally the terms of the peace treaty but also made a friendly agreement with the Yugo-slav Government. The Bulgarian nationalists and Macedonian *comitadji*, in their tribal ideas of Balkan politics, regarded this kind of statesmanship as a betrayal of their cause. They, therefore, rallied to the support of the nationalist government of M. Tsan-kov, a former professor of political economy in the University of Sofia, who was still in office when we arrived.

All this history was in the back of my mind when I paid my respects to the Prime Minister and the Minister of Foreign Af-fairs, and even more strongly when all the Cabinet turned up at a dinner given for me on the evening of the second day. By a happy chance they had escaped the bombing of the cathedral, but here they were all gathered together in a single room, which, so far as I could make out in the dark, fronted on a park and seemed un-guarded. It was a perfect target for conspirators to aim at, and, in spite of the repression of recent months, there was reason to be-lieve that the woods were full of them. One well planned *coup* could have got rid of the whole government. However, nothing happened except a pleasant exchange of after-dinner speeches.

The morning of that day, November 6, was spent in a long talk with young King Boris III. The King received me alone, opening the door himself to admit me to what he called his office, a long room with absolutely none of the trappings of a palace. Its walls were bare, lacking any kind of decoration; there were only two or three office-like chairs and a few books. The most striking ob-ject was on a shelf by the door—a telegraph instrument of the ordinary kind to be found in railroad stations. When I remarked about it, King Boris explained that he had a mechanical bent and had learned how to telegraph when a boy, and that this was very useful to him because he could send messages which the telephone might garble. But he said that it was also the direct access to him from the government officials in the provinces. At that time he said that the last thing he wanted to hear was the click of the in-strument, for it might mean the worsening of the situation in Macedonia.

In this way we at once plunged into a discussion of the most serious threat to peace in Europe since the end of the World War, the border dispute with Greece. The story has been told too often to repeat in detail, although it was by far the most serious international event of those years, for it was only by a matter of hours that the League of Nations prevented a Greek invasion of Bulgarian soil. The King was still anxious, for, to quote his own words, that was a part of the world where guns go off on their own accord.

The Bulgarian account of the incident was a clear-cut statement in the note sent to the League of Nations appealing for intervention: "On the 19th instant, about three o'clock in the morning, Greek soldiers crossed the frontier and fired on a Bulgarian sentinel. . . . The Bulgarian sentinel returned the fire and killed the aggressor, whereupon a detachment of Greek soldiers under post orders advanced into Bulgarian territory to recover the Greek soldier's body. Soldiers of the Bulgarian post opposed this movement before the customary formalities had been fulfilled and a fusillade which lasted until the evening of the 20th instant commenced." The Bulgarian Government claimed that it had ordered its frontier garrisons to make no opposition to the invasion and that subsequently "Greek detachments were able to occupy a number of posts in the Struma Valley and Greek artillery hurled numerous bombs into the village of Petritch and the railway station at Marnopole . . . while a Greek airplane dropped bombs on the village of Levunovo wounding five Bulgarian soldiers."

The Bulgarian Government then appealed to the League of Nations under Article 10 of the Covenant, which guaranteed against external aggression, and Article 11, which empowered the Council to take any necessary action in case of war or the threat of it.

The Greek Government, on its part, held that the shooting had been begun by the Bulgarians and that it had been an unprovoked and flagrant aggression on their part, in the face of which their military commander had been authorized "to take measures he judged necessary for defense and clearing the national territory of which certain points were still occupied by Bulgarian regular troops."

In both countries the war spirit was immediately fanned by extremists. Refugees from sixty Macedonian villages came fleeing over the mountains with tales of the Greek invasion and memories of the horrors of past Balkan wars with all their atrocities. The situation was doubly difficult for Bulgaria because the country had been disarmed by the Treaty of Neuilly (its counterpart to the Treaty of Versailles), and its appeal to the League of Nations for help was all the more effective on that account.

By good fortune, the president of the Council at the time was M. Briand, whose moral authority was very high, and he, sensing the need for immediate action, telegraphed both governments reminding them of their obligation to submit their dispute to peaceful settlement and requesting them to keep their troops behind their frontiers. This appeal stopped a Greek offensive only two and a half hours before it had been scheduled to start. Thus an anxious weekend passed. The Council met on Monday, October 26, approved M. Briand's action, and sent a "stop-fight" order to both governments, with a demand that within twenty-four hours they issue orders for their troops to evacuate foreign soil inside sixty hours. The British, French, and Italian military attachés at Belgrade and Athens were sent by special trains to the scene of action, arriving there October 28 in the early afternoon. Then for the first time in history, the agents of an international body summoned the commanders of both armies and ordered them to carry out the League's instructions.

Eight hours before the expiration of the time limit, the Greeks were back on their frontier. Peace having been maintained, the League sent a five-man Commission of Inquiry to carry out investigations on the spot and determine responsibilities. Finally Greece was obliged to pay Bulgaria an award for damages amounting to about $210,000.

The Concert of Europe was no longer working as in the days

of the old diplomacy for the selfish advantage of any of the great powers; it was working solely for the maintenance of peace in what had long been known as the Cockpit of Europe. Although I had been eagerly following these events, I had avoided discussion of them with government officials, following narrowly the line I had set for myself during the whole journey, not to get involved in current politics. But there was no escaping the insistent questioning of King Boris on the technical details of the League of Nations, which, he said, had definitely saved Bulgaria from invasion. For hours our conversation ranged over the whole field of international politics. In all this the King made the impression on me of a well-meaning young man—he was then thirty-one—who was seriously weighing the responsibilities of a Balkan kingship in the new technical, scientific age. He said that the escape from history in that part of the world was much more difficult than the Western peoples appreciated. The tragedy of his later life showed that this was only too true. But at that time, he was dreaming of leading his country into an era in which peace would be safeguarded by the League of Nations.

I ought to make it quite clear that King Boris's interest in the movement for international peace clearly stemmed from the crisis of the preceding days and not to any previous thinking on the subject, for which there had been little or no preparation in his environment. He had just witnessed an intervention in the Balkans on the part of the great powers different from anything else in history. Previous interventions had always been to stir up strife for the benefit of the great empires of the nineteenth century, whose shadow had dominated all of Near Eastern diplomacy. Now, under the leadership of the League of Nations, the interference in Balkan quarrels had been solely for the purpose of preventing war. There had been little or no change in the government of the Balkan nations, for it was open or disguised despotism in every case. It was a despotism for which the ancient master, Turkey, had furnished a convincing model, for the success of Mustafa Kemal had been closely watched throughout all the Middle East. Yet, without interference in domestic politics, but taking things as they were, the League of Nations had intervened, not for any one nation but simply to preserve peace. I gathered that the King had at first thought it was too good to be true, and certainly his training had never prepared him for this kind of politics. His father had outdone the most tortuous diplomats of his day and had carried the Bulgarians into the World War as an ally of Austria-Hungary, its old enemy, and had fought against Russia, its oldtime protector and friend. Throughout the war years militarism seemed to pay high dividends by extending Bulgaria's frontiers and offering the chance for plundering its neighbors. It remained free from invasion on its own soil, even escaping any air-raid damage. The only disasters it suffered were those registered in the peace treaty, which were accepted as the normal consequences of defeat.

It was therefore not to be expected that the King or any of his subjects would be ready to subscribe to the conclusion which I had drawn from the history of the war, that the nature of modern war had changed under the impact of science because it had escaped control and become a world catastrophe. This horizon of world politics lay beyond the vision of any observers in Sofia. It was only the sudden intervention of the League of Nations which brought home to them the fact that they were no longer free to fight out their quarrels as they had always done in the past.

The King's interest in the implications of this incident seemed to me much more lively than that of his ministers, whose attitude was correctly cordial in the formal and official way. For the King it was evidently a personal problem which was so much on his mind that he spoke rapidly and without any apparent reserve, turning from English to French, in which he was more proficient. He made the impression upon me of a young man who was not sure of himself, but especially well inclined toward the United States because of the contribution of Robert College to the education of the young men of Bulgaria. Had we been in the League of Nations at the time this influence would have been stronger still. Unfortunately, the King's Germanic connections and his marriage with an Italian princess were later to throw him into the camp of the Axis powers. Hitler, however, seems to have been suspicious of his loyalty to the German cause and the sudden death of Boris in 1943 was attributed to Hitler's minions.

The interview with the King was only the beginning of the day's work. The afternoon was given up to conferences with professors, of economics and politics, each of them of the conservative type which made him *persona grata* with his colleagues in the government. Then at six o'clock we were called for by the rector of the University to go over to their largest public hall, which, it should be noted, was that of the *Alliance française*, the great French propaganda agency. There we found a packed house to listen to my lecture before the Academy of Science. There is no need to pause over this last public address of the journey, which dealt mostly with the work of the Carnegie Endowment and the War History. I was surprised, however, to find the next morning that the Sofia papers had reported the event in great detail, as though it were a matter of national importance. Evidently the word had got around that the King had been interested.

It was after this meeting that the dinner was given in our honor, to which I have referred above. By midnight it seemed as though we had been spending several weeks in Sofia, so full had the days been of interest and work.

Next morning, November 9, keeping to our schedule we left Sofia for Constantinople on the Oriental Express. A separate compartment was reserved for us, but it was unnecessary as there were only three or four other passengers in our section of the train. At the railway station we were surprised to find M. Kissimoff waiting for us, to present to Mrs. Shotwell the largest floral tribute I have ever seen on any occasion. He explained that the King himself had ordered it to be sent to her because there had not been time for him to entertain her at the palace. There were so many flowers that it filled one whole compartment. Naturally it made considerable impression upon the conductor of the train.

This was the route from Berlin to Bagdad which the Emperor William had made so much of; I had expected therefore that this particular train, the best one on the road, would be as speedy as any in Western Europe, but going through the Balkan Mountains there were grades so steep that the engine could hardly pull the train in spite of the fact that it was almost empty. There were places where I could have walked or run alongside the track as fast as the train was going. Then, when it got over the divide it speeded down into a valley where we saw water buffaloes at work in the fields, black, big-horned, patient animals dragging along homemade ploughs or pulling lumbering farm wagons along the road. The chief crop in some of the fields seemed to be turnips, and we took snapshots of piles of these in the dooryards of farmhouses. Other parts of Bulgaria are more fertile and the climate more temperate, but the landscapes along the main railroad line offer little to charm the eye.

Night had already set in when we pulled up at a station on the Turkish frontier. Then we had the strangest and in retrospect the most amusing incident of the whole journey. At the time, however, it was by no means a matter of amusement. The train halted a long time while the customs officers went through the baggage of every passenger, going to the bottom of all valises and trunks. When they started in on my own the conductor protested energetically that I had been a guest of the King and government and he showed them my diplomatic *laisser-passer*. This, however, had no effect on the police who continued rifling our baggage until they came upon the signed photograph of the King. Then there was a hurried and excited conversation and they hastily closed everything up with profound apologies. This, however, was not enough for me. I insisted on knowing what it was they were doing and why they had acted in this way, and then the chief of police told me that orders had gone out that day to every frontier station of Bulgaria to watch everyone attempting to cross the frontier because the night before someone had broken into the numismatic museum of Sofia and had stolen the gold coins of Alexander the Great and other rare coins—one of the most precious hoards in any museum in the world. This apparently had been taking place while I was the guest of the government at their banquet in my honor, which they told me was only a stone's throw from the museum.

When we had time to recover we could see the humor of the situation. If the news of the incident ever got back to Sofia we never knew of it.

10 · Turkey

THE GREATEST of all "iron curtains" in history is that which has separated, and still separates, the Moslem from the Christian world. Although from time to time it was partly torn aside by the Crusaders of the Middle Ages, or pushed aside by the trading cities of Italy in the Renaissance, it has remained until our own day the dominant fact in the Near East. This is because religious prejudices, if given rein and not held in check by the sober realities of rational thinking, are the strongest of all impulses, having the strength of the primitive tabu. Throughout history, therefore, the "unbeliever" has been regarded as the most dangerous of enemies, armed not only with a sword, but with a curse to kill the soul. Antagonisms which go as deep as this cannot be shuffled off in time of peace, but continue to block the path of understanding and distort the conception of what the "unbelievers" are really like.

The most striking instance of this kind of misunderstanding is our conception of the Turk. The nation which has been the titular leader of the larger part of the Mohammedan world and its greatest champion in Eastern Europe has now been revealed as the least fanatic of Mohammedan peoples, its head, Mustafa Kemal, discarding almost casually the caliphate, the sacred office of the successorship of Mohammed. Yet this act, one of the most revolutionary in the history of religion, was not inconsistent with the history and traditions of the Ottoman Turk. For the keynote of that history was militarism rather than religion. The institutions of that government and the structure of society were not dominated by the rigid prescriptions of the priesthood, but by the requirements of military science.

Fortunately for the sultans, Islam was a warring religion so that there was no conflict of morals between the secular and religious powers. Islam has no Sermon on the Mount. In using war as an instrument of national policy the Turk never had to struggle with his conscience, as was the case increasingly in the Christian nations of the West. Nor was there anything in his background which would lead him to join in a movement for world peace.

Therefore my visit to Turkey was on a wholly different plan from that to the other Balkan countries. Its purpose was to draw the lesson for the Western countries of the effect of militarism upon the militarists themselves. Throughout the other countries of the Balkans there had been ample evidence of its effect upon the subject peoples, but here at last we were to come to grips with the central theme of militarism itself—a theme standing out more clearly here than in any other country. The effects of German militarism were hard to disentangle from the effects of Germany's prodigious industrial output. The effects of Russian militarism were still harder to trace in the Bolshevik revolutionary movements. But in Turkey the lessons of history were clear, as clear at least as they are ever reflected in the distorted glass of history. For the Ottoman Turkish monarchy was, above all things, the rule of the soldier, the combination of two great militarisms—that of Rome through Byzantium, on the one hand, and of the warlike monarchies of Asia on the other. Concentrating upon the army, the Turks left civilian affairs to a bureaucracy very largely composed of Armenians and Greeks, so long as they were competent and willing to serve their Turkish masters. Religion played little part in this organization of government, the chief interest of which was conquest and exploitation of the conquered.

As in the case of every great military system, the initial stages were those of power and magnificence. Nowhere else in the modern world is this law of history more evident than in the splendor of the creations of the Turkish sultans in the long line of massive domes and slender minarets that crown the hills of Constantinople. There is only one more breath-taking sight in all the world than that from the Tower of Galata, which crowns the hill east of the Golden Horn. It is the view of lower Manhattan from across the

THE BOSPORUS FROM THE WALLS OF CONSTANTINOPLE

SULTAN AHMED MOSQUE, CONSTANTINOPLE

East River at the close of a winter day when all the lights are lit
and the skyscrapers become nothing short of miracles for anyone
with an eye to see. Old Rome, apart from the buildings of the
Renaissance, is a broken shell compared with the monumental
aspect of the new Rome on the Golden Horn. There is more of
the sense of power in the old Roman ruins or in the Forbidden
City in Peking, although this is not lacking in the city walls of
Constantinople which held against so many invasions. But nowhere else in the world is there anything to compare with the
mosques of Constantinople. Rounded arch and soaring pinnacle
were fitted into an architectural harmony, grandiose but jewel-
like in the richness of decoration, and furnishing a link not with
the West, but with the glamorous East. It was a Byzantine Turk
who designed the Taj Mahal.

In spite of its magnificence, however, the Ottoman Empire,
like all monarchies ruled by the sword, had in it from the very
first the elements of decay. Already by the eighteenth century its
age of greatness was over. While this was partly due to the rise
of sea power and the ocean route which cut in upon the oriental
trade, it was a decline inherent in the nature of the Turkish state.
The economics of conquest are those of ultimate exhaustion, for
the exploitation of the conquered calls for no cooperation on his
part and lessens the interest of even the ruling class in the fundamental principles of its own welfare. This is a law of history
which admits of no exception, but its operation is often slow because of many other factors in the evolution of politics. Had
there been strong neighbors at hand or had the European powers
been able to agree among themselves as to the fate of the Near
East, the Ottoman Empire would have been broken up long before it was, for already by the middle of the nineteenth century
the "Sick Man of Europe" was no idle phrase. But the Empire
lived on for a half century more, chiefly owing to the rivalries
of the great powers. Hardly had Russia driven it from its hold
on the Black Sea before the British, as a result of Napoleon's invasion of Egypt, began to take, for the first time, a lively interest

in the Near East. These rivalries played into the hands of Bismarck when, at the Congress of Berlin in 1878, he made himself "the honest broker" of the bazaar of power politics.

All this was ended, however, when in 1912 the subject peoples of the Balkans took their fate in their own hands and showed to an astonished Europe the utter weakness of the caliphate whose sovereignty was still recognized throughout the Arab world. The World War, which for a time had seemed to check the threatened downfall of the Ottoman Empire, ended by registering its complete collapse, leaving to the Turks only the hinterland of Asia Minor.

Here was a theme which fitted perfectly into the scheme of the Carnegie Endowment History of the War, but it was one which could not be handled by any but a Turk who had both a clear understanding of the background of Turkish history and experience of the War itself. For in the postwar years the resurgence of Turkish nationalism had been an even greater surprise to the Western world than the eclipse of the Empire in the Balkan Wars. Judged on the surface of things, Turkish militarism had justified itself in the defeat of the Greek invaders of Anatolia, who had succeeded, by the deft diplomacy of Venizelos, in securing the backing of Lloyd George. The support of the British for the Greek aggression was not backed up, however, by their allies or even by the British dominions, and it was as a successful military leader that Mustafa Kemal consolidated his power at Angora.

These recent events had made an analysis of Turkish militarism an extremely difficult task. Fortunately the qualifications for such a study were fully met by my friend and former student, Dr. Ahmed Emin,* who, as a scholarship student in Columbia University, had taken his doctorate in social science under such great teachers as John Dewey and Franklin Giddings. Dr. Emin had also taken my courses in social and economic history and had

---

*Dr. Emin has added to his name the family surname Yalman. It was in 1935 that the introduction of family names was made obligatory and universal. Mustafa Kemal became Kemal Attatürk (Father of the Turks).

then gone back to Turkey to become the director of a liberal newspaper and a writer on political and social problems. A discriminating critic of Turkish nationalism, he was at the same time a loyal supporter of the Angora regime. I had sent word to him before about my plans for undertaking a study of the unique problem of Turkish militarism. Upon my arrival in Constantinople I found that I could link up the old University associations as though they had never been interrupted by a world war. For his judgments were objective and devoid of any tendency to excuse or apologize both during the War and after.

His volume, *Turkey in the World War*, although it was not published until much later, is but a development of the theme of our conversations during my stay in Constantinople, and both for that reason and because there is no other similar treatment of this subject in the literature that deals with the Near East, I have decided to quote in the Appendix several sections from its opening chapters.

Apart from my visits with Dr. Emin there is not much to record of the visit to Constantinople. There were good talks with Mr. G. Howland Shaw, then the Chargé d'Affaires of the American Embassy and later Assistant Secretary of State (1941–44). Mr. Shaw impressed me very much indeed, by his scholarly outlook and sober judgment, as a man to be relied upon anywhere. There were also visits to be made and lectures to be given in Robert College; these were attended by the students from the women's college, also. These two great American institutions which stand side by side on the hilly slope where the embattled walls of the city reach down to the Bosporus, have—along with the other colleges of the Near East Foundation—played a larger part in the history of that part of the world than most people realize. In a very real sense Robert College succeeded to the old Palace School of Muhammad the Conqueror. The president of Robert College was Doctor Gates but most of the arrangements for my visits were made by the dean, Dr. Edgar Fisher. The American College for Girls, a unique establishment in that part of the world, had been largely the creation of one of the great women of our time, Dr. Mary Patrick, who in the course of her long academic career did more than any other single person for the education of the women of the Near East. Although she had retired the year before, her influence was still dominant in her college. Already the new Turkish nationalism was cutting in upon the work of these institutions and the New Turkish university system was increasingly taking their place.

There is no reason to regret this unavoidable trend because it is part and parcel of the modernization of Turkey, the most dramatic social and intellectual change in the history of any nation. The outward sign of this movement was the prohibition of the wearing of the fez by the men and the veil by the women, a law so strictly enforced that the men and women who jostled each other in the narrow, busy streets of Constantinople looked as modern and Western as the crowds of Paris. A touch of the old customs, however, persisted in the bazaars, where no one purchased anything of value without first sitting down with the merchant to a cup of Turkish coffee. This gave a friendly tone to the inevitable bartering, without which shopping in Constantinople would lose most of its peculiar flavor. The merchants themselves were mostly Greek or Armenian, but that was all one to the Western tourists who purchased rugs or bric-a-brac for not more than twice what they would pay at home for the same articles.

For a while I played with the idea of going on to Angora to talk with Turkish government officials in the same way as I had found so worth while in the other countries. This would have given me a firsthand glimpse of Asia Minor as well; but there were two good reasons for not going. The most important one was that a discussion of the aims of the Carnegie Endowment would have seemed very unreal to Mustafa Kemal and his associates. The thesis that war as an instrument of national policy should be renounced because the final results were not those registered on the battlefield could hardly appeal to a government which only a few months before had driven the Greeks out of their seats on the western seacoast, thus unifying all Asia Minor under Turkish rule, and had secured Constantinople against European aggression by extending the frontier against Bulgaria and Greece.

The argument against militarism would have had hard going in a government which apparently had at least used it to great advantage. In reality, however, the recent wars of the Turks had not been wars of national aggrandizement but of defense. This had been true in the whole long series of wars from 1911, when Italy attacked the Turkish outposts in Cyrenaica and the islands of the Aegean, down to the last victory over the Greeks in 1922. Even the ancient structure of Turkish militarism, based upon maintaining a military caste in power, was lacking in the nationalist levies of the Young Turks, whose aim was no longer that of wars of conquest and aggression, but the defense of a beleaguered fatherland. No theory of international peace can renounce a war of defense. In the eyes of the Turks the Graeco-Turkish War was a pure case of Greek aggression, crowding the Turks out of the lands over which they had ruled ever since their arrival in Asia Minor. Venizelos, on the other hand, had convinced Lloyd George that he was simply applying the principle of self-determination of peoples by giving freedom and independence to the Greek population of ancient Ionia. So complicated a situation did not easily lend itself to the theory of the ultimate fallacy of modern war. For it concentrated upon that part of the problem which had been left unsolved by the British rejection of the Protocol of Geneva in 1924.

Under these circumstances and in view of the fact that it had not been possible to make previous preparations for a visit to Angora, it was decided to turn back home from Constantinople, reserving time only for a visit to the one remaining Balkan country, namely, Greece. Our journey into Asia was therefore limited to a ferry ride across the Straits to Scutari, a suburban town from which to look back across the mile or so of water to

Constantinople and the hills beyond. This view is less impressive than that from the hill of Galata, but in the foreground, beside the massive dome of Santa Sofia, one sees the white-walled Palace of the Sultans standing out from the greenery of its parklike grounds which reach down to the waterfront at the point where old Byzantium stood before the days of Constantine.

I had hoped to be able to travel by day down the Dardanelles and through the Aegean Islands, but the only ship to Athens left at night and there was not even a moon to show the contour of the shore as we passed between the battlefields of Gallipoli and the plains of Troy. It is only a night's sail, however, until the eastern shores of Greece come in sight, and in the hazy morning light of a late November day we scudded around the eastern cape of Attica and entered the harbor of the Piraeus.

11 · Greece

IT IS STRANGE that the country which first gave the world a science of politics should be one of the worst-governed in Europe, yet that has been the condition of Greece throughout most of its recent history. It was even true during part of the regime of Venizelos, whose brilliant handling of foreign affairs was by no means matched by his domestic politics. A government of factions rather than of parties had suffered throughout the decade following the World War from the fact that King Constantine had been pro-German and that after his return to Athens in December, 1920, he had cherished for at least a short interval a dream of the restoration of the Greek Empire. But the war with the Turks ended not only in military disaster but in such intense partisan bitterness within Greece itself that six of the King's chief ministers were shot for treason.

This was the situation which brought to the fore the man who was Dictator of Greece in the autumn of 1925—General Pangalos. After the disaster at Smyrna, when the Greek army was so badly routed by the Turks, the General had, with a small but efficient force, held back a threatened invasion of Greece on the Thracian frontier. His popularity therefore was such that two years later, in June, 1925, he established himself in power by a *coup d'état*. Six months later in January, 1926, he rounded off his *coup d'état* by making himself dictator. In the following August, however, he was overthrown to make way for other politicians forming cliques within the two major parties—republican and royalist— each of which had its short and stormy term of power. This was a situation which lasted until 1939. After Venizelos' last ministry (1928-32) there was little choice left for the Greeks but republican or royal dictatorship. Such in a word was the historic background of the problem of Greece.

The Greek people themselves, although traditionally avid for politics, had been described to me both in Geneva and the other Balkan capitals as so worn out by war and factional fight as to be more or less indifferent to the changes in the form of government at Athens. This appraisal was heartily shared by our Minister at Athens, Mr. E. B. Laughlin, with whom I discussed the matter at length on more than one occasion. While his comments were judicious in temper, he felt that he could speak frankly with me and it was from him that I learned at first hand of the intrigues which made up so large a part of Greek political life. A man of modest demeanor, quiet and reserved in manner, he represented the best traditions of the American diplomatic corps, shrewd in his judgments of men and affairs and able to keep his counsel even under trying circumstances.

Studying the situation from the vantage point of the Legation, he had drawn some fundamental conclusions as to the effect of government or lack of it upon the people themselves. With the intermittent spells of tyranny and anarchy, the people, especially the younger generation, were showing the effects of anarchy in a boisterous individualism. When I complained about the tooting of automobile horns all night along the main street of Athens in front of our hotel, he smilingly produced a small box of wax stoppers for the ears which he said he had found necessary if he were to have any sleep at all, for the automobilists were using the great thoroughfare almost like a race course, driving recklessly down the middle of it and raising clouds of dust from the sections of it which were still unpaved. Pedestrians had to jump for the sidewalk for safety as the Model-T Fords or the Renaults came dashing along. There was one thing to be thankful for, however, and that was that the horns were not the shrill metallic products of Germany, which have since led the world in dissonance, but the softer French horn blown by pressing a rubber bulb and producing a note that was halfway between suppressed hysteria and the mournful lowing of distant cattle. Even this alleviation of the noise, however, was little appreciated, as it kept up hour after hour all night long.

In short, the impression I had when arriving in Greece, an impression not changed by my short stay there, was that with its economic poverty and its political feuds it had become the most backward of the Balkan countries.

This, however, did not hold true of the Greek intellectuals at the University of Athens, where a small but notable group of scholars were holding their own among the elite of European savants. Fortunately for me this was especially true in the field of economics where Professor Andreades had made a place for himself that ranked with the leaders of economic thought in the universities of Western Europe. Before my arrival I had been in correspondence with him and had secured his consent to undertake the direction of a series of studies of the economic and social effects of the World War upon Greece. With his accustomed energy he had already drawn up his program of studies and secured collaboration from five of his colleagues so that within a few days we had completely worked out the plan for the War History of Greece.

Unfortunately there is not much to be said of this volume, for it was hard to disentangle the data of the World War from the other wars which Greece had fought almost constantly from 1912 to 1923. Moreover, the confusion was rendered greater still by the lateness of the Greek entry into the World War (June, 1917) and the fact that the Armistice of November, 1918, brought no lessening of military operations on the part of Greece. Nevertheless Professor Andreades and his colleagues prepared a careful statistical survey of the cost of these wars to the Greek people, the only survey of the kind that has been made.

The one outstanding result of war which was most evident to the Greek people was the vast influx of refugees fleeing from the Turkish victories in Asia Minor and Thrace. This came on the heels of refugees in the Balkan Wars and the World War until there were at least a million and a half refugees for whom homes had to be found in poverty-stricken Greece. American and English philanthropic help, although extremely generous, was utterly inadequate and finally in 1923 the League of Nations set up its independent Refugee Settlement Commission and secured a loan under an international guarantee.

The settlement of these refugees, whose newly built little homes sprinkled the countryside around Athens and in many other parts of Greece, lay outside the scope of our survey. Fortunately, much was written about them both in the official publications of the League of Nations and in the United States. It was the largest single enterprise of its kind in history and, upon the whole, remarkably successful. The Ionian Greeks from Asia Minor brought not only new techniques to the mainland, but a new vitality to the population. At the time of our visit it was the one encouraging fact in Greek economic life.

I had made it a point to keep my visit to Greece purely unofficial, limiting my contacts to the academic world, having no desire to link up acquaintance with politicians in any country, but one afternoon I accepted what Professor Andreades said was an informal invitation to tea with the Foreign Minister, M. Roufos. To my surprise there was a formal ceremony in his apartment at which he told of my official reception in the other Balkan countries and ended by conferring upon me the Commandership of the Order of the Redeemer, a distinction which I would have appreciated much more if it had not come from the government of Pangalos.

Modern Athens is a disappointing city. It is saved from the commonplace only by the fact that one is always conscious of its historic past and of the monuments of its ancient splendor. The only touch of beauty along the modern streets is the long row of stately palm trees out toward the royal palace, an avenue not rivaled anywhere except in Hollywood. The University section, in the plain between the old city and Mount Lycabettus on the east, is laid out in unimaginative squares like the new sections of any Western town, and the University buildings, good in their way, are not distinguished. If it were not for its antiquities modern Athens would take a very secondary place among the capital cities of Eastern Europe.

But even in ruins ancient Athens is a living presence that cannot be put by. Here and there in the city itself, one comes upon fragments of ancient buildings and monuments like that of Lysicrates, pathetically out of place in an atmosphere utterly foreign to it in every way. Fortunately the ground around the Temple of Theseus has been cleared so that the city does not intrude upon it. But when one turns the corner of the street from it, one is at once back in the commonplace city of today.

It is the Parthenon alone which compensates for the disappointment to the traveler in the city of Athens itself. Rising five hundred feet above the plain, the rocky escarpment of the Acropolis is crowned by a creation to which no description in any language has ever been able to do justice. One has to see the Parthenon to appreciate it. Surrounded by the cracked stones of its ruined walls and peristyle it still remains a greater monument than any other in the world. In one respect at least it is possibly more beautiful than in the days of Pericles, for the white marble of Pentelicus, however richly veined, must have been too dazzling in the Athenian sunlight. Now the fluted columns have mellowed to a softer tone which blends with the shadows of the architrave. Like all great art it imposes silence upon the beholder.

Strangely enough this world of Pericles had as direct a bearing upon the understanding of the place of war in history as any study of the world today. For the Parthenon itself, like the mosques of Constantinople or the palaces of ancient Rome, was a trophy of war and exploitation. Nowhere else in the world was the fallacy of war as an instrument of politics more clearly shown than in the history of Greece. Yet no one was aware of its ultimately disastrous effects, even when crowned with victory. The greatest work in Greek history, that of Thucydides, takes war for granted as the main interest of the state and records little else than the politics of militarism. Nowhere in his pages is there any reference to the social and political evils inherent in such a system and neither Plato nor Aristotle in their textbooks on politics show any awareness of the final tragedy of militarism. In the light of today this is a distinct limitation in Greek political philosophy, but no one—certainly not the tutor of Alexander—was daring enough to challenge what seemed like a law of nature. Yet as a result of the First World War and the founding of the League of Nations this is exactly what Nicolas Socrate Politis, greatest Greek jurist and statesman of the postwar period and associate of Venizelos, had been doing at this very time in his writings on international morality from Paris and in his contribution to the Protocol of Geneva.

So far my visit to Greece had been entirely limited to the city of Athens. As the work had been very absorbing there I had only two free days for excursions to the historic sites outside of the capital and I therefore saw only the countryside over to the Gulf of Corinth and a section south of it—a poor country in every sense of the word. There were some olive orchards here and there and a few vines and gardens but, except for pockets now and then, farming had practically been given up because of the rocky soil. The stony farms in New England are fertile in comparison. As we were motoring through the Peloponnesus the unproductive landscape became positively depressing, and then suddenly, looking at the map, I realized that we were in Arcadia! It was a world almost entirely deserted, only a shepherd's country like stretches of Scotland, but without its greenery. At one point some distance off the road, I saw a shepherd watching his flock seated on a stone and holding in his hand what seemed to be his shepherd's pipe. For one moment it seemed as though we had suddenly come upon a touch of genuine romance, for here was the shepherd of Arcady. I stopped the car and went over to him apologetically with my camera and started making motions explaining to him that I would like to have a picture of him and his flock. He smiled pleasantly back at me and said

GREEK REFUGEE HUTS NEAR THE FIELD OF MARATHON

AT THE END OF THE JOURNEY

in good American, "That's all right, I came from Brooklyn!" He had been one of the Greek volunteers in the World War, but had neglected to arrange a passport for his return and was by no means happy not to be able to exchange Arcadia for the streets of New York.

The ruined monuments of Greece seem to fit naturally within this rugged landscape as though the destruction of ancient civilization had been part of a cosmic process. Of the Temple of Eleusis nothing is left but the bases of a few columns uncovered by the archeologist, and standing on the spot it is almost impossible to realize that it had been a center of pilgrimage for the Greeks, almost like an ancient Lourdes, and that the religion of the mysteries had furnished the transition to Christianity in the antique world.

If Eleusis had been disappointing, Corinth, a few miles farther on, was a complete surprise, for I had not remembered ever having read that the citadel, Acrocorinthus, that crowned the isthmus of the Peloponnesus was on a precipitous height rising almost nineteen hundred feet above the sea. The ruins of the city itself spread over the plain some distance back from the waterfront. But one would never guess from the few remains which are left that the walls of the ancient commercial metropolis of Greece had had a circuit of ten miles. The Corinth of today is only a slum-like village of one or two thousand poverty-stricken inhabitants. It is, however, a good site for the building of the cottages for the Greek refugees, because there are cultivable fields of relatively deep soil even within the precincts of the ancient city. The chief asset that nature supplies, however, is the surplus water from the various springs, especially the Fountain Peirene, famous in Greek mythology as the spot where Athene helped Bellerophon to bridle Pegasus, and mentioned by Euripides as the place where the Elders of the City were to be found. It is only since 1896 that the excavations at Corinth, begun by the American School of Classical Studies at Athens were dug through to the floor of the ancient Agora and the Temple of Apollo. But the monuments are less impressive than the total aspect of desolation due not only to the ravages of time but to an earthquake in the middle of the nineteenth century. It was after this catastrophe that New Corinth was built in place of the old, the port at the head of the Isthmus of Corinth, some three and a half miles from the ancient city.

From Corinth we turned down to the land of Agamemnon by the Gulf of Argos where the ruins of Mycenae and Tiryns stand out over the Argive Plain. History is full of paradoxes but there is none greater than this—that the walls of the Pelasgian palace, built almost a thousand years before the great age of Greece, have, although in ruins, kept their touch of native majesty next to the Parthenon itself. Although the citadel of Tiryns is re-referred to in Homer and the Cyclopean walls of Mycenae were always visible against the hillside, their massive formation protected them against marauders. This was our last glimpse of the monuments of Greece and it was almost as though the traveler in England had gone from Winchester to Stonehenge before leaving for America.

The next day we took ship for Italy from the harbor in the Gulf of Corinth, and from Brindisi by express train traveled straight to Paris and to Cherbourg for New York.

Appendix I

LECTURE AT THE UNIVERSITY OF BELGRADE

October 9, 1925*

THE FIRST THING that strikes the American traveler to Yugoslavia is that in spite of all the geographical and historical differences between Yugoslavia and the United States, there are some surprising similarities. While the Balkan Peninsula cannot be compared with the vast stretches of the American continent there are sections of it which remind the American traveler of parts of his own country. There is, especially, sunny and beautiful Dalmatia, a miniature California along the shore line of the Adriatic but with at least one city which nothing in California can rival, the jewel-like ancient republic of Dubrovnik (Ragusa). The mountain regions themselves, while resembling no other in Europe or America in geographic formation, have bred a race fully as conscious of the love of liberty as the pioneers of the American wilderness. In addition to this, both peoples are ardently attached to the democratic way of life which, in turn, carries with it a love of justice and of peace based upon justice.

Throughout the centuries, however, the Serbian people, and the other Balkan peoples as well, have had to accept the overlordship of the Turkish oppressor and to live under a government based upon militarism. Escape from this age-long condition could only be by way of force, and the recent history of the Balkans has naturally been that of almost constant wars of liberation.

*As this lecture was given extemporaneously (see p. 61), the text is drawn from two sources: the account in the leading Belgrade newspaper, *Politika*, and a translation back into English of the stenographic report of the Serbian translation made by Professor Vladata Popovits of the University of Belgrade.

From this fact careless readers have drawn the conclusion that the Serbian people has a special inclination for war. I myself remember hearing a lecturer once say that the Balkan peoples fight constantly because they love war. On that occasion my friend, Professor Michael Pupin, your countryman who honors America as well as Serbia by his magnificent contributions to science, rose to protest indignantly that there was no more peace-loving people to be found anywhere than the Serbs. Their wars have been forced upon them, he said, because there was no other way that they could achieve freedom. This judgment is one favored by all thoughtful students of Balkan history but it also is a challenge to the present and the future. For after freedom has been won, its only safety from domestic tyranny as well as from foreign aggression is the development of justice within the democracy and of the structure of international peace among nations.

This at once brings us to the central challenge of our time. How can the politics of peace be made effective?

One thing must be clear at the start. There is no solid basis for a lasting peace in mere pacifism of the sentimental type. Self-defense is a foundation not only of justice but of peace as well. If this were not broadened beyond the defense of the individual and of his family to include the defense of his country as well, it would mean anarchy. But in the defense of one's country one becomes a partner in that long process of stabilization and of the growth of government in the future which welds a nation together.

In saying this I have in mind especially the unforgettable experience of yesterday, when I made the pilgrimage to the grave of your unknown soldier. You have placed it yonder on the height of proud Avala, looking over the battlefields where the Serbian army held back the Austrian invaders in the opening months of the World War. No Egyptian ruler had a nobler setting for his grave than this Serbian soldier at rest on this mountain top, high over the hills and fields which he defended. In the presence of such sacrifice and mindful of the motives which animated the defense of freedom, nothing should be said against patriotism by those who are the advocates of peace in the world today. Lasting peace must recognize that ancient virtue, but must build beyond it, with reference not only to experiences of the peace but also with regard to the actual circumstances of the world of today, for the conditions of life are rapidly changing, more rapidly than ever before in history. In our own lifetime they have changed more than in all the previous thousands of years of history. Scientific discoveries are remaking not only the world around us but time and space, the two essential factors of life. Time is almost completely annihilated. Now in less than a minute we can flash the news across the surface of the earth. The newspaper of today picks up the news from far off Australia more quickly than formerly it traveled from one editorial room to another in the same building. The old post wagons have given way to railroads and airplanes. Isolation is rapidly disappearing, and the frontiers of nations are no longer the same, no matter how we fortify them against invasion. It is impossible to escape the unifying force of science.

When I was in Perugia, that beautiful city of the Italian Renaissance rising on a hill above the valley of the upper Tiber, I could see in the distance the monastery of Assisi, the home of Saint Francis. There on the horizon lay one of the greatest spiritual centers of the Middle Ages. But within the Perugia monastery itself there were agricultural implements from Germany and the United States, for the cloister had become the distribution center of an agricultural college. In Rome the electric lights shine in the Coliseum, and they have tunneled the Hill of the Quirinal.

It is in this connection that we must now study the data of modern war, for the revolution in human affairs produced by modern science has changed the nature of war as well as that of peace. This is the greatest revolution in the history of politics, for war has been the dominant factor in political history. It is older than history itself. It underlay the change from tribal life to political organization and was used at every turn of the development of civilization. The State, that supreme achievement of the forces of human cohesion, was founded by war, and developed through war its capacity to protect culture and even religion. The warrior and the priest have been the two chief leaders of humanity out of the condition of barbarism into what we call civilization. The sword has played a part almost as decisive as the altar in creating those conditions under which humanity can advance from one level to another; and practically at every turning point in this evolution, war has been the deciding factor. It would, at first sight, seem impossible that such a fundamental element in our history could ever be got rid of.

As a matter of fact only one other institution whose history resembles that of war has been suppressed by the conscience of the modern world; I refer to slavery.

Slavery is as old as war. In the history of early civilizations it played a part that seemed to the people of those ages absolutely necessary and essential. The culture of antiquity was built upon it; the splendor of Greece rested upon the labor of the slave; the civilization of Rome was brought to it by the captives dragged at the chariot wheels or herded in the vast slave quarters of the princely Roman estates. Slavery was accepted and even sanctioned by the dominant religions. You who read your Plato for the high ideals of the antique world, or to whom the stoic virtues of Marcus Aurelius make their appeal, find it hard to realize that these masters in the progress of human ideals accepted the institution of slavery as a natural and inevitable human fact.

Now what happened to slavery? It was finally abolished (at least legally) when modern science placed at the disposal of the civilized world implements to supplant human labor for the world's work in commerce and industry. The inventions of machinery and the progress of practical science gave to culture a basis other than that of slavery. So, in the eighteenth and nineteenth centuries, it was possible to suppress the traffic in slaves, against which the Church, representing the organized conscience of mankind, had long but ineffectively protested. If one reads history deeply, one sees that in these supreme movements religion and science are not antagonistic, but that science can furnish means for the practical realization of the ideals of religion.

The movement to rid the world of aggressive war is very similar to that which has already rid it of slavery. Christianity has made a similar protest against war. But until the present, the practical means for realizing this ideal have not been found. Perhaps it would not have been discovered in our time if it had not been for the World War. For that war revealed the fact that war itself has changed in nature. In the past, every war had been regarded as a part of national policy; it was the final argument—the *ultima ratio*—in international controversies. The threat of war was the power behind diplomacy. Statesmen planned to use the potentialities of their "striking forces," their army or navy, as a natural function of the state. War was controllable; at least in a master hand it could be directed to attain certain ends. It might now and then turn out differently from what the statesmen had expected, but that could happen to any human plan. In short, prior to the World War, war itself could be conceived of as a relatively controllable phenomenon. The World War showed that this controllable nature of war no longer exists. War is now like an explosion taking place in the midst of highly intricate machinery. It travels in directions that cannot be foreseen, for it involves interests of other states not party to the original conflict. It spreads like a contagion from country to country, and though some may escape, no one can tell beforehand the extent or direction it may take; any more than anyone can tell beforehand who may be the victim in a city stricken by the plague.

Speaking in this city and in this hall, it is unnecessary for me to remind you how much the World War itself was due to the fact that statesmen of the Central Powers believed they could "localize" the conflict. It spread from these hills of yours to the most distant corners of the earth, not alone because of treaty obligations, but rather because the real and vital interests of these distant lands were endangered. The World War revealed that there had grown up between the nations an interdependence in economic life, the extent of which had been unsuspected hitherto. We think of nations as having the geographical frontiers of their country. But the financial frontiers are not those shown on the map. Many nations in the world have their financial capital in London, Paris, or New York; commercial nations have a common interest in foreign ports. With the development of modern machinery there are countries whose very life depends upon the markets they can find for their production in other lands. This overlapping of national interests has developed to such an extent in our time that it is impossible any longer for even the greatest nations or the strongest powers to be entirely self-sufficient as they formerly were, before the emergence of modern science.

It would take many lectures rather than these few sentences to give an adequate picture of that new thing which the modern nation has become, when it enlists the forces of Nature to do its work, and alongside its living human population creates vast new numbers of working hands in iron and steel.

But I have said enough to indicate that the new nature of war, as revealed in the World War, was not a mere single chance event but was the inevitable consequence of the new character of civilization. If this is so, war cannot be treated as in the past by responsible statesmen. It cannot be held down to achieve a single purpose; it is impossible to calculate its consequences, and the statesman who uses it henceforth as a proper and natural instrument for the attainment of policy is not only playing a dangerous game with the lives of his fellow countrymen and the fortunes of his state, but he is, as well, involving many other nations in the same fate. The new, vast forces of the economic world confront him—and cannot be adequately foreseen.

In the last analysis, modern science, in creating new conditions of peace, has created new conditions of war. In addition it has made war itself more terrible. The next war, if there is to be one, would be supplied with poison gas and airplanes sufficient to wipe out all the chief centers of civilization. I know of a single factory, of one company alone, which could in a short time be so transformed as to draw from the nitrates in the air above it (mixed with a few other things) a thousand tons a day of high explosives; enough produced in one day to destroy utterly a city of this size. I surely need not do more than refer to this destructive power, which would in the next war be used against the civilian population and not merely against armies.

The reason we are to get rid of aggressive war is simply because we must. If civilization cannot check war, war will destroy civilization. The first step, therefore, has been to reach an agreement among the nations that aggressive war is itself a crime. This agreement was actually reached between governments at Geneva (including your own) a year ago. But how can one define aggressive war? Most wars of aggression are camouflaged as wars of defense. It is not the nation which first crosses the frontier which is necessarily the aggressor. There is no military test that will be final and set. Here, therefore, a seemingly impassable obstacle presents itself, for it is of little value to declare aggression a crime if there is no way of detecting the aggressor. The dilemma was solved this last year by a new definition originally proposed by an American Committee, then advanced by the Prime Minister of France, Monsieur Herriot, at Geneva, and accepted now by all the great powers of Europe. It is the essential basis for the guarantee of Britain in the pact of security now being negotiated between Britain, France, and Germany. In the words of Monsieur Herriot: "The aggressor is that power which *goes to war, refusing arbitration.*"

This is more than a definition. It is a demand for a substitute for war; without a substitute, war will go on. The substitute is an appeal to justice.

But this at once brings up the question whether one can get "justice" by an appeal to a tribunal. Certainly not in the eyes of the disputants in many cases; but, if each contestant insists upon his sovereign rights and will not yield to what an impartial third party decides, there will be no progress whatever towards justice for anyone. Progress in justice has consisted in the bettering of procedure. The willingness to abide by decisions, even when these are unsatisfactory, has been the indispensable condition for the evolution of any of our systems of justice within the state. The same must be true of international affairs. As we have learned to regard that man as a criminal who insists upon asserting his own claims in defiance of the decision of civil courts, so we shall have to regard that nation as a criminal which insists upon asserting its claims against others when international tribunals of justice pronounce against it.

We are only at the beginning of international justice and it can only come in proportion as the sovereign states learn that they must give up some portion of their sovereignty into the hands of international tribunals as the condition of their existence.

But if we are to have peace we must have more than arbitration for the disputes which arise in international affairs. We must deal with those affairs before they develop disputes. Peace is not simply the avoidance of war, it is a condition of life. It must be organized as war has been; it covers first of all the intricate mechanism of economics and world culture.

There is no time to develop this great theme. But here above all is the challenge to the coming generations to solve. It will be their great opportunity to build out of these separate city states in which we live today a real federation of nations. The need of defense against attack will remain for generations still to come. The menace of war must be faced during the period of change. For long years to come soldiers must still protect our heritage. But under the new regime, they will be soldiers of peace rather than of war. Like the science of medicine which has developed from the cure of diseases to their prevention, so the soldiers of the future will safeguard our security as in the past, without provoking aggression; and so the noblest attribute of their profession will thus be preserved.

In closing, let me ask you to take what I have given not as a new gospel to be made over into an accepted creed, but rather as a subject for our further serious thought and a challenge to the intelligence of those to whom this civilization is worth preserving.

It is in this way alone that we can carry on the work of those who gave their lives in the World War—and in many a war before that—in order that their home and country might endure.

Appendix II

A TURNING POINT IN HISTORY*

WE ARE LIVING at a turning point in history. This era which has witnessed a World War is also witnessing the beginning of a still greater historical event, which is nothing short of a movement to rid the world of war as a political instrument and to make aggressive wars between civilized nations an international crime. I am not speaking of wars of defense nor of peoples that are not civilized. Naturally, a movement so cast as this is one that affects the world, one that reaches down to the foundation of human society; but, while its effects are world-wide, in our time, its hope can hardly become a reality except among those peoples whose mental growth is such that they can work together with understanding and with that sense of security which rests upon mutual trust and honor. I do not believe that we can think of war as ended forever; but I do believe that we now see aggressive war shaken by the most powerful of onslaughts, onslaughts too which do not at the same time strike at war of defense. For if there is to be no war of aggression, it follows that there would be no need of defense.

What grounds have we for believing that we are to see a change so vast and so profound in international politics? We can answer that question most easily if we will give a few moments to the evidence of how far we have got, even by now.

Down to very recent times, war—and war of every kind—was one of the wholly legitimate prerogatives of the sovereign state. Indeed, in its power to declare war lay sovereignty's inherent proof and token. And this has become one of the first principles

*Translation of the address at the Institut Social de Bucharest. See p. 101.

of international law. If you ask for a proof of that, simply turn the pages of any handbook of international law written in the eighteenth or nineteenth century. Take, for example, Vattel's treatment of the matter in his *Law of Nations*, the manual which during the last century was most generally in use. There you will find it set down that the state, the modern state, the sovereign state, is in time of war the sole judge of its own actions as it is in times of peace. Sovereignty's symbol lies just in this, that neither in its relation with other states nor with its own does there exist any superior power by which sovereignty can itself be judged. From this it also follows that if international law allows liberty of action in time of war, and if all diplomatic relations have been based upon such liberty of action in hours of crisis, the state is entirely free to strike at its adversary, to work its will by force, and to put no curb upon its power save the limit only of its own desires. The one measure of the might of a state has been the strength of its armed forces. Sheltered behind them, its diplomats met those of other states and with them considered how best they could bring to fulfillment what they deemed to be the needs of the world, viewed internationally.

International law, diplomatic law, law veritably founded on the freedom of engaging in war—no one could even dream of calling it in question.

Behind this conception of sovereignty was an historical movement. For when a modern state was made a reality, something more took place than the mere embodiment of an ideal suddenly bursting upon this world. As you, above all, are in a position to know, behind the creation of a modern state was the whole historical current of things, the entire history of Europe. And history makes it plain that, at every critical epoch, war had been the true agent of realization. Nor has this been true only in the case of modern states. Consider the great French Revolution. It was by war that it imposed its results on Europe, that it affirmed the rights of man. It was war that fixed our present frontiers. War, working in the very bosom of states, has created sovereign power, the strength of nations, and won nations their liberty. In human history war has always been the *ultima ratio*. It is as if, when it came to matters of international policy, there had to be full freedom to levy both upon the wealth of nations and upon the lives of their people. In history, then, the part played by war has had an importance which history itself has not always realized at its full. That being so, can we be at once a good historian and such a revolutionist as to believe that the civilized world will suffer itself to be deprived of a tool that is so useful? Are we to take the impossible position that after having made full use of this war tool to establish liberty, to secure democracy, and to create our modern states, we are now to throw it aside and forget it ever existed? How could we ever do without so valuable a thing? It is only too plain that we are here in a position that would at least seem impossible; and I doubt if the world has ever seen its like before.

But there is even more to be said. For war has been not only such a tool in modern times; it has likewise existed from the beginning of history. It came into being before any other human institution, before law itself. War is older than civilization. It has endured throughout all the history of civilization. Very well, but for all that I believe we are going to make an end of aggressive war!

Moreover, there is one thing which may give us courage. If you will turn back into the pages of history you will find that the abolition of slavery—which was merely one step in the progress of modern civilization—was something which the people of antiquity felt to be quite unimaginable. It is even impossible to conceive of antique civilization without slavery. Remember that the poets, the thinkers, the philosophers, the great creators of art and science in antiquity all accepted slavery as something established from the beginning—as an institution that was essential, for upon it was based the whole development of the arts and sciences. Plato, with his dreams of the future, Aristotle, with his world views of life and civilization, all those philosophers who in the centuries that followed inspired our dreams of social change and revolution, all alike, when they dreamed their dreams of reform, accepted slavery as its natural background and support.

During the first centuries of Christianity the Church of the Middle Ages set itself, not against the institution of slavery, but rather against the conditions under which it was carried on. True, from time to time, there appeared priests or prophets who saw in slavery itself a thing to shock the Christian conscience. But until the eighteenth century no real effort was made to abolish it. And not until our own time was it brought completely to an end.

What actually freed humanity from slavery? If you look into the matter closely, yet at the same time keep the needed breadth of vision, you will see that in the eighteenth and the nineteenth centuries, when the slave trade was suppressed, the movement which was then at work was not one inspired by religion, although it came to the aid of religious thought. It was a movement of liberation that was bound up with the daily work of man. That movement of liberation was called science. We had begun to master the forces of nature, and we did it to make those forces work for us. Without knowing it, without seeing the connection between these two great questions—slavery on the one hand and modern industrialism on the other—that was how humanity brought slavery to an end.

I believe, indeed, that what we see here is simply the working of a general truth that can be explained and stated in a phrase: call it the progress of modern intelligence seizing upon the forces of nature and substituting them for the labor of man. This at any rate is certain. The movement which ended in the abolition of slavery in the United States had the closest of connections with the industrial development of the North.

Now, today, no one in the civilized world believes that slavery is still necessary—I speak of legal slavery, not of other kinds. Yet slavery was none the less a human institution which had its roots as deeply in history as war itself, an institution perhaps more essential than war, for by it was performed the world's daily labor; an institution which made it possible for the world to make its civilization secure, while war was at least a transient thing. It broke out now in this quarter, now in that, and its results could be forgotten.

Look into the role played by war in history and you will find a parallel which holds true even in details. War, like slavery, goes back to the beginning of human institutions; like slavery, it has fought with the growth of science, for science has changed the human relationships upon which rest both the day's work and the polity of nations. Moreover, just as practical science brought substitutes for labor, so its destructive inventions bring substitutes for the ancient ways of waging war. We are therefore at a point in human development in which science promises to rid us of the ancient institution of war just as it has been the most efficient factor in ridding the world of slavery. In short, human intelligence is a more humanizing element than anyone would suppose who thought of it only in terms of its battle with the forces of nature. The triumph over nature is now revealing itself as, at the same time, a triumph over that primitive barbarism which has remained with us from the period when life itself was a crude and often losing struggle with those forces now within our control.

I believe that the Great War marked a revolution not only by the manner in which it extended itself over the entire world, but by its demonstration that a change has taken place in the essential nature of war, whether carried on by armies or navies. We have been brought up in the belief that war was an instrument that could be used at will to bring this question or that to a settlement, that war was an instrument that we had at all times under our control. The World War has made it plain that the high progress made in this science which kills has taken war of today out of human control. If you look into the preparations that are being made for future wars—and such preparations must be made so long as we can find no substitutes for war—if you are following the progress made by physics and chemistry, by the airplane, by poison gases, by explosives, you will find yourself forced to admit that the science of war has now so perfected itself that it is capable of destroying not only the most determined of enemies, but also our very civilization.

Let us pause long enough to note in detail just what science can really do today. There are factories now in existence which can do two things: they can extract nitrate of ammonia, in thousands of tons, to fertilize the country's farm land, and they can likewise produce explosives in quantities no less enormous, explosives having as their base the inexhaustible resources of air and water, explosives which when dropped by aircraft could in the shortest possible time wholly destroy an entire city. And in the next war it would be not merely the armed forces but the civil population as well that would have to be attacked. For it is above all in the laboratories of universities and the workshops of towns and cities that war is now prepared. The next war will be a war of extermination, since whatever nation is attacked will be compelled to make use of this same kind of chemical warfare in its own defense.

If this be understood, we need go no further to make it clear that science is about to change all our previous conceptions of war, and that the World War marked a turning point in the history of war.

Can we prevent the use of such methods in war? That is as if we asked, Can we block the progress of science? No. Nor can we limit the production of fertilizers which make rich the soil. The thing is impossible. Those same scientific processes may make life easier for us, may mean bread in abundance for everyone. But by these very processes, particularly necessary today when everywhere the World War has left with us such misery, the factories, with very minor changes in apparatus, can turn that which adds to life into civilization-destroying explosives. The same scientists, with the same formulae, can make both things in one and the same laboratory. I remember, for example, visiting an establishment where, during the war, poison gases were made—I have no need to tell you where. In the laboratory next to that in which those poison gases were made, other chemists were at work to save life, and they were using almost the same formulae. The raw materials which went into the manufacture of the tools of death likewise served for the protection of life. One destroyed; the other cured. Before I go on, too, I will say that it was those same scientists, at work in this institution, who discovered the formula for the remedy for sleeping sickness; and it is quite possible that by doing so they will save as many lives as were lost in the recent war. I say it again, those two laboratories were side by side, and the men of science at work in them were availing themselves of the same methods.

That is what science can do. It is something that is stronger than we are. In the history of war we have reached almost the same point which, in the history of slavery, we reached half a century ago. But here the competition with science has results that are far more serious. We have arrived at a place in history where we must choose between the destruction of civilization in its entirety and the possibility of making secure the happiness and well-being of the nations by the abolition of aggressive war.

By now, too, we can reckon up the gains we have already made. The first of these may be said to have been a general agreement that it is not possible to abolish defensive war. For that matter, every modern war has in one sense been held to be a defensive war; every country had claimed defense for its part, has fought only in defense, and has refused to admit that it might be the aggressor. It became necessary, then, to begin by setting up some sort of impartial tribunal to determine who was to be called the aggressor. Modern countries, with a jealous sense of their own sovereignty, had no great desire for such a tribunal. They argued that it would constitute an impeachment of their sovereignty. Accordingly, then, something else had to be found, not a tribunal, but some kind of definition, a definition which, accepted beforehand and by everyone, should automatically indicate who the aggressor was. It was very hard to make the distinction called for, or to put it in scientific terminology—to isolate the microbe of aggressive war. Indeed, from the military point of view, it is not possible to make any distinction between defense and attack. For instance, if a few kilometers from your frontier there rises a hill which dominates your side of it, will it constitute an aggression on the part of your neighbor if, upon that hill, he establishes armaments capable of destroying all your towns and cities within reach or of making easy an invasion of your territory? Looking at it in another way, can we conceive of any statesman, responsible for the safety of his country, who under such conditions would not feel it absolutely necessary to take precautionary measures? Or, to take another instance, must we wait until an enemy's airplanes are on the way to launch their tons of explosives upon our cities? Every expert knows that against airplanes the only defense of any value is to attack them before they are on the way.

I speak as a realist, and I am compelled to recognize the fact that self-defense sometimes makes it necessary for us to be the first to attack. This opinion is everywhere accepted, if not by the general public, then at least by those to whom the safety of the country is entrusted. The military world is therefore at one in admitting that it is frankly impossible to make any distinction between aggression and defense that can be expressed in military language.

What, then, could be done?

The League of Nations took up the problem some two years ago. It did not succeed in reaching any practical distinction; but it did nevertheless lay down one broad general principle which will be the foundation stone of our future law of nations—the principle that aggressive war is a crime.

There we have a declaration which struck at the very bases of that international law whereof I have been speaking to you in the present lecture. To declare before the whole world that aggressive war was a crime was a new thing and a big thing; for, until then, it had always been proclaimed that all states had the right to make war.

At the same time to declare that war was a crime was going only part way, for that was a quite different thing from defining aggression. And to solve this problem we, in America, sought to find a formula. In fact we threw on the table a formula that was revolutionary. We said: The aggressor is the country that goes to war while refusing arbitration, the country that refuses to submit its case to a tribunal, refuses to avail itself of the pertinent means which in time of peace it had agreed upon as well fitted to set such differences right.

To put one's hand upon the aggressor, then, was no matter of learning who was first to cross his neighbor's frontier, but of learning who would refuse to lay his cause before a tribunal of arbitration or other pertinent body. Here too we have something that is more than a definition. It is a demand that war shall be replaced by something else. That is, it is the virtual finding of a substitute for war. As such, and at Geneva a year ago, it was first accepted by Ramsay MacDonald, the Prime Minister of Great Britain, and Edouard Herriot, the Prime Minister of France. Then it was adopted by the representatives of the governments forming the Assembly of the League of Nations. And now it forms a part of the Protocol of Geneva. Indeed, a week ago at Locarno there was signed an agreement which is like the dawn of a new day for Europe and the world. And if you will read the text of that agreement, there too you will find the same definition and conception of aggression. You will see that England gives its guaranty as between France and Germany if such a situation should arise between them as we have been envisaging. If a war situation should arise between those two powers, England has given her word that she will herself go to war against that power which refuses to submit a dispute to peaceful settlement or to comply with an arbitral or judicial decision, while resorting to the use of force instead. In like manner France and Germany each guarantee each other against any violation on the part of other nations unwilling to avail themselves of the processes of arbitration and conciliation.

That is the new conception which made possible the pact of Locarno. From now on, among the great European powers and without any argument, the aggressor will be he, I say it again, who will go to war refusing arbitration.

This is the progress that has been made possible by a new thought, a new conception. Not that this means that the question has been settled absolutely and for all time to come. But it does mean that the first step has been taken. Even if the great powers accept this conception there will still remain many obstacles before we can apply it. Above all it calls for a wholly new kind of education in the science of statecraft.

I have pointed out that hitherto it had been made a principle both in the practice and the theory of statecraft that every state was the one judge not only of its right and freedom to go to war but likewise of the justice of its cause. Can such rights be given up? Can any country renounce them and entrust them to others, to neutrals, to those that we do not feel are as well qualified as we are to judge of the justice of our cause? Are nations truly ready to accept this formula, or will they be when they are facing a crisis? Only think what the thing means. The formula of Locarno —that formula which was behind the Protocol of Geneva—demands that in place of going to war we accept the judgment and the sentence of others.

I admit that this method of settlement will not give a great power that hope of winning its case which it might be given by force. I will even admit that if a country accepts the formula of Locarno, very often it will lose its case. What will seem only justice to others, will not seem so to it. So that a country may well ask itself, Is it truly necessary to accept this definition of aggression? It is, yes, if we are to have peace, for it is the first step in the control of war itself.

As you see, the problem leaves a situation that is still far from simple; and new problems are constantly arising.

However, once more I ask you to look into the pages of history. Those of us who think that justice is an absolute thing should read history. For human justice is always imperfect and relative. *Our* justice, the justice that we accord to others, the sort of justice that others accord to us, none of these things is a justice which is absolutely just. I ask the question of you who are here present: in your own lives have you always obtained that justice which you felt was due you? Absolute justice?

There is no such thing as absolute justice in human affairs. The most we have been able to do is to create an instrument which can be made a safeguard against the abuses of power, against crimes that have been recognized and defined; we have that safeguard in our tribunals, which we then call tribunals of justice. We have set up systems of law by which we seek to make live, at least once in a while, the elements of justice. If we insist upon obtaining absolute justice—that is, the sort of justice we demand for ourselves—we shall simply find ourselves going back to the war conditions of uncivilized tribes. If, however, we are willing to yield a little, we shall yet work out a system that will give us, other things being equal, the maximum of justice. That is the history of civil and criminal law.

Well, the same sort of development must take place among nations. We must be ready to say not merely that that nation which goes to war refusing the services of the Permanent Court or of the Conciliation Commission is a criminal. We must likewise be ready to admit that this criminality shall be followed by the same consequences as in private life. If nations at war can be differentiated, if before all the world we can point out which is the victim and which the criminal, we can then set up some system of justice which will really be a substitute for war. And the whole history of jurisprudence teaches us that progress lies in the establishing of the tribunal and the trying of cases rather than in the enunciation of fine principles. I do not know if I have made myself clear. But read history and make your own comparisons with conditions as they are today, and you will see that we are now at the beginning of an international movement which is almost the same as that social movement which brought about the creation of those local courts before which the citizen learned to lay his case.

If this is true, the definition of aggression is a thing that is much more than a mere definition, for it gives us the right to hope that we may sometime be able to bring aggression to an end by building up the institutions of justice itself.

You see what I conceive the situation to be. That is what has been done at Locarno, at Geneva, and at The Hague. We are looking for the thing that will take the place of war.

The first obstacle we encounter is the challenge to sovereignty, the fear of the modern state that it will no longer be free to make war even when it feels it must protect itself or defend the justice of its cause, the fear that it may lose at one and the same time both its freedom and its security by being thus compelled to resort forthwith to the instruments of peace.

I am not a pacifist in the old sense of the word. I believe there is no peace movement that can hope to succeed if it does not admit the legitimacy of self-defense. I believe in the right of the individual to defend himself against the attack of others. I believe in his right to defend his family, his fireside. And I believe in the right of defending one's country. It is a right which involves not only all the natural feelings of human society; it also constitutes a basis for the safety of future generations. It is impossible to conceive of the success of any peace movement that does not take into account this necessity of self-defense. It follows, too, that if defense cannot be distinguished from aggression we shall always have war. But on the other hand, if we can bring aggression to an end there will no longer be any need for defense.

The process which brings wars of aggression to a close in the world's history is a long one and may extend far beyond our lives. During that process the need for defense will continue. Defensive wars, then, will occur in direct proportion to the number of aggressive wars that violate the process of building up a peaceful world. These defensive wars may be thought of in terms of police action, wars to safeguard the world's gains as it moves toward peace, and to protect the treasures of civilization in the interval.

If you grant the possibility of such wars of defense (or police wars), they, too, may be and almost certainly would be looked upon as aggressive by the other side. I admit this difficulty and agree that it is not enough merely to define aggression and brand it as a crime. It is not enough to state our ideals in terms of a single formula. We must likewise apply the experience of history. The great lawmakers of Rome did not find it enough to lay down definitions—although no definition can ever surpass that which defined justice, in the opening words of the Institutes of Justinian, "Justice is the fixed and constant purpose which gives to every man his due." Definitions such as this were not arrived at by philosophic reasoning; they could not be reached until history itself had revealed and tried out a fixed and constant process for the attainment of this end. The phrase was the crystallization of experience. The jurists were registering achievement, as well as indicating an ideal.

In the same way, our present generation has reached certain general ideas as to the possibilities of peace and the outlawry of aggressive war. But it will not be until years have passed, and until future generations have done much blind groping, that permanent peace will finally be won. I am not one to be discouraged, if now here, now there, wars still break out. Murder still continues, although there is a law and there are courts designed to prevent it. It is only by experience that we can reach the solution of any difficulty. It is not by invoking untried ideas, but by the hard and obstinate work of responsible statesmen, who at every step will have to determine if the time has come to apply a new solution to the situation there facing them; it is only by their action that the result will be attained in its finality. With the passing of time, and always more and more, we shall find in our international tribunals the true instruments of justice and of peace.

I do not believe that it is enough to say, as it is so common to say, in the United States, that war can be blotted out by Permanent Courts. They are not enough, because the majority of questions which will lead to war are not the legal irritations which arise between countries. I believe accordingly that our definition must be made more subtle, more malleable, and at the same time strong enough to be able to take hold of all sorts of diplomatic obstacles, such, for example, as those that may arise outside of international law. That this need not be difficult is very well illustrated by that formula which is at the very center of the pact of Locarno. We must bring together both elements in international relations, the elements that are political and the elements that have their source in codes and courts. But all that is only a question of time, of experience.

To make an end, I believe that the movement toward justice is already sufficiently far advanced to constitute an historical phenomenon. I believe that this generation, which has gone down under a catastrophe without parallel—this generation which has suffered as no other has ever suffered in the past—can serve the cause of peace—peace reached by the paths of justice—with more fervor, with more intensity, than any generation in the immediate past or future. In any case, it is our duty so to do.

I went this afternoon to that spot where lies the unknown soldier of your army, and before his grave there came back to my mind the undying words of our Lincoln, those words spoken by him upon the field of Gettysburg, "that from these honoured dead we take increased devotion to that cause for which they gave the last full measure of devotion; that we here highly resolve that these dead shall not have died in vain." The cause for which they died was not only that of the safety of their country but that of peace through security. I see this security as a thing henceforth safeguarded not merely by the instruments of war, but much more by the growth of justice. For if, as I have said, from now on war will be no longer under the control of men, then it will not safeguard us, and in its place we must put something which will be under our control. The time when war was a weapon which one could use as a safe means for insuring our lives, and the life of our nation, is gone; today war is like an explosion, and an explosion that must recoil upon the nation which lit the fuse.

For five years I have had the task of examining the economic and social effects of war throughout all Europe. I have no need to tell you that such a task has uncovered for me economic and social effects of war in every country, both belligerent and neutral, which make clear how great a menace is modern war, a menace not only to the institutions of liberty which have been won by the effort and sacrifice of so many generations, but no less a menace to that heritage of culture, of art, and of creative science which is the basis of our civilization. But greater than all the loss of wealth there is another, which above all we must not forget. That is the loss of lives. Have you ever thought what that loss of life in the late war was? If all those soldiers who fell could rise from their graves, could take rank again, four deep, in their regiments and companies, this army, a spectral army but a real one, would extend, in its columns of four, from Constantinople to Paris. All these lives have been sacrificed, and sacrificed, I think, for something!

Who, among statesmen, will in future dare to take upon his shoulders the responsibility of a new war, when it is possible to save so many lives for the Fatherland by the adoption of principles in international affairs such as are merely those we make use of in the home affairs of a nation. That may seem, too, to be making no very great change; but in truth such a change would carry with it one of the greatest revolutions in history. Can we bring it about? That is the question that our generation must face.

Appendix III

THE FLIGHT OF THE SERBIAN PEOPLE
IN THE AUTUMN AND WINTER OF 1914*

THE MOST VIVID picture left by the war in the memory of the Serbs is not of a cemetery or a blood-stained battlefield, although Serbia had given a formidable number of victims and had been the scene of the fiercest fighting. The most clear-cut impression of the Serbian campaign is the motley, pitiful spectacle of the "bejaniya," that endless, disorderly flight of fugitives muffled to the eyes, old men, women, children, on foot or in wooden carts patiently drawn by emaciated and exhausted oxen, driving in front of them some cattle and carrying on their backs or under their arms some chattels, the number and importance of which grew less with every stage of this removal which was always beginning again and never coming to an end. In short, the outstanding event of the Serbian war is not a great battle, such as Verdun, but the Great Retreat, that retreat which led the Serbs into exile through Albania—the last after so many others following on each advance of the enemy.

This flitting began the instant the Austrians first bombarded the town of Belgrade and the terrified villages of the Matchva and those on the banks of the Save and the Drina. With every advance of the enemy—especially after the cruel deeds of the Austro-Hungarian soldiers were noised abroad, in August, 1914 —the inhabitants of the villages in the regions occupied by troops, whether Serbian or enemy, thronged the miry roads, those famous Serbian roads, unequaled throughout the world for potholes and

*Translated from *Les Effets économiques et sociaux de la Guerre en Serbie*, by Dragolioub Yovanovich, pp. 28–38. Cf. p. 62.

mud, journeying whither they knew not. "You could see two or three rows of these crude, heavy and ramshackle carts, drawn by a pair of oxen or cows, overloaded with goods and bedding, on which sat children looking with tearful eyes on the slowly moving crowd. Over the sides hung pots and pans, crocks and vessels; fastened by ropes to the back of the cart walked poultry, sheep, heifers. The animals in harness were led by boys of fifteen to eighteen; the old men and women carried foodstuffs and the mothers had infants at the breast. Here a broken-down cart would hold up the whole of this living column, with its long medley of men, baggage, and cattle. After a shorter or longer delay they would go on journeying, day and night, through the autumn rain. Wet and cold nights became more and more common and death began to remove babes, women, and exhausted old people. In the darkness of night soldiers hewed a way through these hapless beings, soldiers of the Serbian army hastening to arrive punctually at the posts allotted to them. Night hid the tears which poured from the eyes of these war-weary, suffering soldiers, passing close to their wives and children without daring to utter a word lest they should let their children know that their father was going away, leaving them to slavery."

.　　.　　.

But the martyrdom was as yet incomplete. After the retreat through Serbia, every soldier and every refugee, man and woman, on arriving at the frontier of the national territory, had to make his choice: to remain under Austrian and Bulgarian occupation or to risk crossing Albania and Montenegro, to end—where? The soldiers were naturally not consulted as to which road they wished to follow, but it has been proved that almost everyone could make a free choice. . . . It was the second half of November. The Serbian army was still in possession of the mountains between the Sitnitsa and the Drim. Preparations were already being made to plunge into Albania. Soldiers and refugees—henceforward a joint band—were preparing for the terrible journey through the wild countries of Albania and Montenegro. On all sides, horse carriages and ox-wagons were turned into handcarts, which alone were capable of traversing the tracks and bad Albanian roads. The country round Petch was turned into a huge workshop. Each driver became a blacksmith for good or ill. All the unwanted parts of the carriages were at once put on the fires which were already burning because of the early frosts of the district. The dry wood of the racks and the wheels gave an excellent fire, and the shaft, after years of tarring, made a dense smoke which rose to heaven in a thin quivering spiral. There were countless numbers of these smoke columns round the wonder-stricken town of Petch. Along with this work of transformation, they also went on to destroy all the artillery and ammunition wagons, except for a few which were to be taken across Mount Jlyeb and Montenegro toward the Adriatic.

All this swarm made its way imperceptibly by the southeast slope of Jlyeb toward its summit. There were numerous roads leading there. Wherever water flowed from the summit to the plain there was a path, and a living stream of men and wagons passed along it. No order anywhere: while artillerymen grew hoarse shouting at the countless and overworked horses, certain refugees seated at the side of the road looked on calmly at the hubbub, quietly eating the last remnants of the provisions they had brought from home. From below, in the depths of huge precipices, arose the intermittent thunder of munitions thrown in the fire. All along the road, shells and hand grenades lay on the ground: foot-soldiers picked up the bombs, only to drop them farther on when too tired to carry them.

Often the journey was beautiful, with lovely air and glorious views. Under other conditions this journey would have been unsurpassed for enjoyment. (Many refugees will remember afterward the natural beauties of this district and will feel a desire to return there, but of their own wish and with their knapsacks differently equipped from 1915!) Heavily clad, overburdened with belongings, they all quickly tired climbing the very steep slope: sweat rolled down their faces and bodies. They had to make frequent stops. The clear blue sky urged them on to walk, but the hot sun beating down on them brought fatigue and weariness. While some sat down to rest, others got up to continue their journey; thus it went on for several weeks. Soldiers and refugees were attired alike: many soldiers wore a hat or cap of sheepskin instead of a helmet; in contrast many women had their legs clothed in officers' breeches and on their heads a kepi with a cockade; others even wore jack boots. There a mother, bent under the weight of a child on her back, walks with difficulty, breaking under fatigue; there another woman, unburdened, well dressed, is seated on a mountain pony, which paces slowly, snuffling into the neck of its guide, the tender husband walking with sweating face, open mouth, and swollen eyelids. . . . The nearer they got to the summit the nearer the mountain ranges appeared to each other. From the base of the mountain there seemed to be endless ranges, at first countless, then reduced to merely a few. . . . The first terrace was laden with four-wheeled carriages, drawn by oxen. Men had pushed them as far as that by dint of cries, oaths, and curses. Then they waited, for what they knew not. Some had already begun to turn their carriages into carts. . . . Such a huddle of carriages, carts, pack-beasts, soldiers, refugees, made movement slow. They could not stir, forward or backward, out of their rank. One thinks of the procession of the faithful approaching the altar to make their communion. . . . At last they arrived at the spot where met all the roads and paths from the base. Such a huge crowd was gathered there that movement was almost impossible. Each had to wait his turn to pass on. Sometimes they stayed at this spot for ten, fifteen, twenty hours without moving. Shovings, cries, oaths never ceased. On the other side of the ravine they entered a defile which could only be traversed in single file. All the troops of three armies had to go through this narrow passage. At the entrance to the defile leading to Rojay were those in charge of the crossing—mostly commanding officers of divisions or armies. Each officer sought to get his own troops, and even his baggage-train, through first, from which arose misunderstandings which only hindered the march: no one would budge till the argument was settled. This put in a rage those who had been long waiting. On all sides could be heard insults, cries, deep sighs, lamentations: "Never shall we get away from here!" and "God of our fathers, whither hast Thou brought us?"

Weary of waiting, some decided to turn back a little to get some rest apart. They made a way for themselves with difficulty through the crowd which got denser and denser. Night drew on and a thick fog enveloped all. From the base of the mountain to the entrance to the defile the slopes were thinly covered with stunted beeches. Thousands of fires, with which the countryside of Petch would be covered for several weeks, had been lighted then on the huge side of Jlyeb. This ever-barren mountain was now swarming with life. Never had it worn a more solemn appearance. Its usual denizens, the bears and wolves, had retired before these undesirable guests. Before entering the ravine which led to the defile an ox-wagon stood at the head of the stationary file. The beasts stood motionless and looked stolidly at all this crowd of soldiers and refugees. Ill chance had made them, too, leave their dear Matchva and brought them to these rocky and wild mountains. When asked why he did not give his animals any food, the driver replied, "I would give them plenty of food if there was any. I can only give them these beech branches, since there is no more grass. I've been here for some days and have given them all I had in the way of food; I'm stuck here. Luckily there is plenty of water." Everywhere there were fires, which the fog put out a little, and all around huddled soldiers and refugees. Some never ceased telling their story, others remained silent looking at the red flickers of flame. . . . This strange encampment took on a more peculiar aspect by reason of the thin childish voices which could be heard here and there. The cry of "Mother" for a moment stifled one's sorrows and brought back one's thoughts to the peaceful, happy life of the family circle. These voices also awoke in some the remembrance of their own children left behind them, at the mercy of the black unknown. . . . But night went on, the fires became fainter and fainter. Round each fire the weary travelers lay sleeping in the abandonment of relaxed effort. In each group a man watched over the fire. From the side of the defile the noise never ceased; all wanted, if not at once, at all events as soon as possible, to get clear of this spot, especially as the moment for doing so seemed to be farther away instead of nearer. Voices rose from below, from beside the town with its circle of encompassing fires, the voices of those who were hastening to reach the ravine and get nearer the fatal defile; they had continued to march through the night. From time to time the human voices were drowned by the bellowing of famished oxen and the terrified cries of asses; the relative peace of the night was disturbed by them. Those who for the first time in their lives are sleeping on branches, with a small bag of biscuits for pillow, jump up and make as if to get ready. A moment after they fall back mechanically into the same posture. . . .

Vainly did they try to enter the defile, day and night; every slope and terrace stayed filled with men and beasts, from the foot of the mountain to its summit. . . . When at last his turn arrived to move, every man passed the defile at a run. Once across, he made the sign of the Cross, saying, "God be praised, we have gained the threshold of Paradise."

Far from being a paradise, it was only the first stage of a Calvary which was to endure for several weeks. They were still in Serbian territory. Down below in the thick fog, in the midst of a huge plain, curving over the Drim like the hump of a camel, the refugees could see a bridge—a bridge which marked the frontier between Serbia and Albania. "With every fresh step we took we felt ourselves nearer to losing the last corner of our free territory. Like those condemned to death, we first counted the days left us to live free, then the hours, then the minutes. It seemed to me at first that we were marching too slowly in flight before the enemy, then it seemed we ought to hasten, lastly it seemed we were marching too fast. . . . Gently, gently, let us not leave in such haste this last hundred yards of free Serbian land! . . . A little further on, when we are on the banks of the Drim, our blood-stained fatherland will be already behind us, and in front of us will be the distant and unknown paths of sorrow and suffering. . . . This bridge which we are crossing now—would it not be right to call it, too, the Bridge of Sighs?" The poets express what the common man feels but vaguely and cannot express. "By the waters of Albania, by the waters of Death," wrote later M. Jiv. Dévétcherski, "we halted our soldiers. By the waters of the Chkoumba, Séména, Voyoucha, we halted to rest our bones. Alone our bones were left us, our bones, death and honor on the flags of glory. . . . We buried under the willows our blood-stained standards, and we sat sad and miserable, at the time of the zenith without sun, on a day of holy festival without rejoicing. We were laid low on earth, but we wept not at all, we died in silence, as a great mourning is silent—silent like the Great Passion on the Cross at Jerusalem. . . ."

Appendix IV

TURKEY IN THE WORLD WAR*

A LONG CAREER OF WAR

THE *Background of Conquest.*—The World War did not mean for Turkey a break in stable peace conditions. It was the culmination of a long series of wars, in which she had taken part, first as an aggressor, then as an object of aggression. In the beginning, the ruins of the Seljukian and Byzantine empires formed a kind of empty frame which the efficient Turkish war machine rapidly and successfully filled; and then in its turn the ruins of the Ottoman Empire became a possibility which whetted national appetites, and constantly threatened the peace and stability of Europe.

We can discern in the past of Turkey an ever active process of growth and decay. To the men in power in Turkey in July, 1914, the World War seemed to be, first, an exceptional chance not only to end the undesirable and undignified rôle Turkey had so long played, that of merely so much booty, to be divided in this way or that, as the Great Powers might see fit; second, it seemed to be a chance for Turkey once more to become the aggressor. And the attempt to regain that rôle, so out of proportion to her resources and equipment, ended in the total collapse of the ancient Empire. The Turkish Republic of the present should be looked upon as a new life, which came into being two years after the Sick Man of Europe had passed away.

The social and economic conditions affected by the last war were at the time in a state of change and flux, and bore the im-

*Extracts from the volume, *Turkey in the World War,* by Ahmed Emin, in the *Economic and Social History of the World War.*

prints of a chaotic career of war that began in the past. The effects of the Great War can be much better understood if we begin with the records of Turkey's earlier history, and study its general character and trend. . . .

The founders of the Ottoman Empire migrated westward from Central Asia in the middle of the thirteenth century. They were driven from their homes both by the Mongol invasion and by a long period of drought. Asia Minor, misruled both by the Byzantine Empire and the Seljukian Turks, discontented and depopulated, attracted them. After they had separated, for various reasons, from the main group of fifty thousand Turkish immigrants, they formed only a small group of four hundred tents, or two thousand souls.

They were good soldiers and good shepherds. They followed a simple mode of life. In religion they were really shamanists, and Mohammedan only in name. The whole country, up to the western and northern coastal regions, had been Turkified by the Seljuks two centuries before they came; and the peasants of the country, embittered by the misrule of their Byzantine landlords and priests, readily embraced the religion and language of the handful of nomad conquerors. . . .

There was the same anarchy in both adjoining empires [the Byzantine and the Seljukian]. While the great landowners in the Empire of the East looked to the Church to maintain their sway over the oppressed and mutinous masses, religious fanaticism had, as a result of the Crusades, become the dominant feature of the Seljukian Empire. Its economic situation was also no better than that of its Christian neighbor. In this frontier borderland between, two forces had been turned against them, those who had been made to suffer either in purse or conscience, and those who, knowing themselves capable and deserving of advancement, could hope for none under the corrupt rule of either empire. And both those forces were drawn to the just and liberal system of government of the first [Ottoman] "Sultans." . . . Every variety of religious opinion was tolerated, and also atheism.

The Machinery of Conquest.—The machinery of government, planned and worked out for the new empire, was one which could serve only when any former dogmatic authority or vested interest could wholly be ignored. It might seem in fact the off-spring of some utopian spirit, and no system that, for any length of time, could ever be made to work in real life.

Its main purpose was conquest, for, as has been said, the vast territories on either side formed a kind of empty frame. They were lands that asked to be given order and rule. At that time, the beginning of the fourteenth century, they would have tempted any organized and ambitious government. And the force that was to conquer and rule them was evolved and got itself together.

What was needed, it was felt, was a standing army with a permanent system of recruiting and supply; and the army that was put in being was marvelously organized. It had been so planned that for a backbone it could be given a yearly levy of youths who, non-Turkish in blood, could be carefully selected and rigorously trained in special institutions. To quote from Sir Edward Creasy's *History of the Ottoman Turks* [page 15],

"Cut off from all ties of country, kith and kin, but with high pay and privilege, with ample opportunities for military advancement and for the gratification of the violent, the sensual, and the sordid sides of their animal natures amid the customary atrocities of successful warfare, this military brotherhood grew up to be the strongest and fiercest instrument of imperial ambition, with remorseless fanaticism, prompted by the most subtle statecraft ever devised upon earth."

. . .

As the consequences of this system, the Sultan was the only real power in the country; he had no rivals even of the second or third order. He ruled at the head of his Turkified slaves who, though for the most part of specialized training, were parts of a strictly organized and intricate machine.

There were few chances for favoritism in public life under such circumstances, and anything resembling an hereditary aristocracy, outside that of the imperial family, was little tolerated. Political and religious refugees of mark and talent, coming from any corner of the world, always possessed a good chance of preferment in Turkish public life. There were great opportunities for the inventor; for every idea which promised to be practical was most highly prized. That may explain why the Ottoman Empire was in technical equipment always ahead of its time, and benefited by the use of gunpowder before the rest of the world.

The Turks themselves formed, seemingly, a class bereft of privileges. Careers in the army or governing circles were all but closed to them. Of the forty-nine grand viziers who came to power between 1453 and 1623, only five were Turks; and even these held office mostly in the latter part of the sixteenth century when the original system had already been shattered. Eleven were South Slavs, eleven Albanians, one, an Armenian, one, a Georgian, one, an Italian, one, a Circassian, and eighteen belonged to various other outside races. Every possible language was spoken in the Sultan's train. Even the sons of new converts—who at once took rank as Turks by birth—were debarred from public life. The general object seemed to be to keep the great mass of the population from aspiring to become creatures of the Government, and to force them to devote their energies to commerce, agriculture, manufacturing, and to the learned professions. Such an arrangement, of high value to the internal development of the new empire, also contributed greatly to the absolute autocracy of the Sultans, for it kept any influential political groups from growing up.

The community life of non-Turkish races went on without interference.

The Ottoman Empire . . . formed a happy contrast in this regard to the contemporary world. The Slavs were not oppressed as in Greek times. There was no trace of the German anarchy of the same period. Inspectors made their rounds four times a year to see that the non-Turkish peoples were well treated. For them there was a change in just one thing that affected their everyday lives: The great landowners were now of a different race. The Turks paid cash for all they bought. The man who stole a chicken from a peasant made himself liable to the death penalty. In every way, indeed, it was recognized that without such a reign of law, it would be impossible to hold territories where the majority of the inhabitants were Christians.

The Imperial Government.—Broadly speaking, the Ottoman Empire had, in its time of growth and rise—from 1299 to 1566—many of the characteristics of a modern government. It pursued its various policies, military, political, economic, and social, with a full knowledge of existing conditions and a clear perception of the main object to be gained. Statistics as to population, housing, occupation, live stock, revenues, and military matters—all were carefully kept. Much thought and attention was given to military and political affairs in the foreign world. And the study of history and geography was encouraged.

The standards of living and of public health were much higher than those of Europe in general at that time. Foreign ambassadors in Turkey often showed the same envious admiration that is felt today by the Turk traveling in Europe or America, when he observes the working of Western public institutions. In so far as sanitation,* cleanliness, regularity of food supply, and a constant struggle against the high cost of living could go, city life was in good control. It was one of the ordinary functions of state to maintain free caravanserais, or inns, for strangers, and free public kitchens, hospitals, asylums, and libraries. There were many opportunities to obtain a free education.

Government aid and encouragement were lent to manufacturing, commerce, and agriculture, and they were protected from all unlawful interference. Skilled immigrants, no matter what country they came from, were given many kinds of assistance. When

---

*For example, such establishments as tanneries had, for sanitary reasons, to be built outside the city walls.

some center of industry was captured, some of the artisans taken
were sent to the home territory of the Empire. When Selim I
took Tabriz, an important manufacturing town at that time—
1512—he brought a thousand such workmen to Constantinople as
a sort of present. Nor were problems of population in general
lost sight of. After the plague of 1466 many of the inhabitants of
Dalmatia were sent to Constantinople to make good the losses it
had suffered. When, in 1475, Geodosia was taken, five hundred
Latin families were sent to the same destination for the same purpose.

Much careful consideration was given to matters of home and
foreign trade. When the first vessels of the Turkish navy were
built, in 1462, they were built with the express purpose of protecting Turkish commerce. . . .

Agriculture was highly advanced. Not only did Asia Minor
feed Turkey, the Aegean Islands, and Greece; it was also Italy's
chief source of supply, so far as wheat was concerned. One of the
means of putting pressure on the Italian states was to threaten to
cut off their wheat imports. And a bad harvest in Turkey meant
much suffering for Italians.

Economics and Religion.—The economic and social situation in
Turkey up to the middle of the sixteenth century is well expressed by a phrase of Professor Patten's. Her position was one
of "surplus economy." And all historical phraseology might gain
in clearness, if for "Orient" and "Occident" were substituted such
terms as "surplus" and "deficit economy," which would really
bring out the character of existing conditions in a given area. If
such terms were used it would become quite clear that static
social groups are mostly associated with deficit, and dynamic
groups with surplus economy. Before the full advent of the commercial revolution in the West, the Turkish Empire formed a dynamic group, although geographically it was situated most largely
in the Orient. It would be wrong and misleading to speak of
stereotyped conditions as peculiar to any fixed geographical area;
there are everywhere reactions to the sum total of the existing

stimuli, a change in the stimuli causing corresponding changes in the reactions. Every environment and period has its own religion, as part of its general equipment of existence. Words like Christianity and Islam may denote a common source of some of the general dogmas respectively in force, but cannot give any idea of the special character of religious life. "Surplus economy" brings about a religion of the successful, who treat the divinities on an equal footing, while "deficit economy" tries to supplant by religion the material possessions that are wanting, it makes itself humble and obedient to supernatural forces, and has an influential priesthood.

In the period when the Ottoman Empire was waging successful warfare, Islam was a religion well adapted to the viewpoint of the successful warrior. It had a certain ceremonial value, and acted as insurance for the after life. Not that, when drunk with success, its sons gave much time to thoughts of the after life. And in the Turk of that time there was no trace of fatalism. Ill fortune was not humbly accepted as a punishment sent from heaven for unknown sins; with promptness and energy steps were taken to change the course of destiny. Religious bigotry, an outstanding characteristic of the period of national decline, was ridiculed; and everywhere people took a broad and liberal view of life. . . .

Religion, as a reason for making war, played almost no part at all. Campaigns against neighboring Mohammedan states were not less frequent than those against Christians. And even when it was a case of two hostile camps ceaselessly at war, they were not divided along religious lines. In spite of the constant pressure in Europe to launch new crusades and bring about a united European front against the supremacy of Turkey, one of the rival groups in Europe was always seeking to obtain secret or open understandings with her. On the other hand, coöperation with the Mohammedan enemies of the Ottoman Empire invariably formed part of the plan of action for the complete and final defeat of the Sultan.

The Empire at Its Height.—The outstanding object of war was conquest. The Ottoman Empire was in the position of sole heir to both the Seljuk and Byzantine possessions. And when they had been won, that brought new appetite for conquests in all directions—Syria, Egypt, Mesopotamia, Persia, the northern shores of the Black Sea, Hungary, Greece, Bosnia, and the African side of the Mediterranean. The Aegean Islands were seized for the defense of the Empire and for the purpose of protecting coastal trade. And Turkey had to wage wars of defense as often as her foreign enemies came to believe there was good opportunity for reconquest and revenge; for instance, when the Empire was suffering from internal troubles, or when a strong Sultan had passed away.

The state of war was the normal state. Any state of general peace was the exception. The existence of a standing army with a perfectly organized supply service, and capable of making the business of war a very profitable one, was often the real cause of war. The costly machine insisted that it be used. With that there were other incentives, the desire for adventure and booty, for example, and the high rewards that were paid for individual deeds of daring. The lust for war was there; and peace-loving Sultans such as Murat II (1421–1451), Bajazet II (1481–1512), and—at times—Suleiman the Magnificent (1520–1566) were hard put to it to keep that war-loving standing army under due subjection.

The cost of waging war was too great to make it profitable in itself. The Empire's regular revenue, drawn from economic sources, had to be lavishly spent for it. The long wars in the time of Selim I and Suleiman (1512–1566) had been made possible by the economies of Bajazet. And he had managed to maintain twenty years of uninterrupted peace only by enduring foreign humiliations, provocations, and the discontent of the military classes. Only when a war ended with the conquest of a rich province could the revenue therefrom compensate for the expense incurred. . . .

The net gains from the Ottoman Empire's career of successful warfare, which lasted nearly three centuries, was some 2,000,000 square miles of territory containing a mixed population of 50,-000,000, speaking twenty different languages.

This territory was too great for further expansion, and the machine of government too artificial to maintain its old efficiency forever. An era of decline was bound to follow this excessive growth and those moral consequences of abundant material success that accompanied it.

WAR BECOMES A LOSING BUSINESS

The Price of Aggression.—There is a limit to every imperialistic growth, for the price paid for aggression is a very high one. Incessant wars leading to abnormal expansion absorb the resources of the home country, throw away the fittest and most courageous elements of the population, and make so many claims upon the spirit of self-denial and self-sacrifice that in time they can produce only returns that grow ever less. Moreover, the factor of increasing distances begins to work against the conqueror. The burden of policing a vast and heterogeneous population becomes heavier and heavier, and the defeated are in the end led to unite in self-defense.

The skilful masters of Ottoman statecraft had made many provisions to meet the natural elements of decline. It was thanks only to that that a light artificial scheme of organization, selection, and training could be carried on for two and a half centuries. And when of necessity the end came at last, the breakdown was immediate and complete.

The Break-up of the War Machine.—By the seventeenth century the tremendous power of the throne, which in the time of the Empire's growth was the steadfast guardian of the public interest, had fallen to nothing. While the Sultans amused themselves in their harems, three several influences began to struggle for the power they had lost, and all three were narrow and selfish enough. The first was the organized brotherhood of janissaries, the second the ulema, or the country's religious teachers and judges, and the third was made up of the different cliques of palace women. In addition to these elements, all struggling against each other, either separately or in semi-alliance, there was always a vast amount of personal intrigue at work.

The janissaries, chosen as children from non-Mohammedan communities, in a sort of settled blood tax, had once been a force under high discipline, and one of the chief instruments of conquest. When the decline set in, their training was abandoned as a measure of economy. Youths of fifteen and sixteen were taken instead of children of six and seven. Furthermore, the Turks revolted against the old order of things which put them aside to the profit of the recruited Christian boys; and in their revolt they forced their way into not only this military caste of janissaries, but into all those offices which had been virtually closed to them for two hundred and fifty years. At the same time the janissaries, now mostly native Turks, grew in number from 30,000 to 60,000. At the beginning of the nineteenth century, there were 400,000 of them, though only 25,000 were in actual military service. And the janissaries were no longer the advocates of war, for the probability of defeat was now far greater than it once had been. Since, too, they no longer had that easy source of booty that once had lain in war, the Sultan, the treasury, and the populace became their victims. Every new Sultan had to make their caste a "gift" of not less than 2,500,000 ducats, while both government and people were entirely at their mercy. The majority of them had, in addition to their nominal positions as soldiers, a secondary profession. They were merchants, artisans, firemen, and beggars. But, each and all, they acted the part of bands of brigands who were above the law.

From time to time the debauchery of the Palace led to temporary returns to decency. At such times the influence of religion began to assert itself, the general feeling being this: "The country is going to ruin. It is hopeless to seek to stop it by the forces of this world. God must be our refuge." And the representatives of religion were, of course, ready to play their part. But they put a heavy price on their intervention. They insisted that the highest law authority in the religious world should be consulted upon every detail of state activity, including even the making of war and peace, and the appointment of governors, army commanders, and state officials.

Neither the army leaders nor the palace women found this to their liking. Both alike declared that religious teachers should stay by their books, and do no meddling with state affairs. In 1602, there were serious clashes between the powers of religion and the army. In spite of such opposition, however, all real power began more and more to pass into the hands of the ulema. The Ottoman Empire, once the abode of freedom of thought, and the embodiment of the complete victory of reason over authority, became a blind theocracy; that, too, just at the time when Europe was beginning to free herself from such bonds, and develop as seemed best to her.

Every new invention, every project or idea that was new had been welcomed in the time of the Empire's growth and greatness. The mollahs who ruled in the era of decline were against every sort of innovation. Only such tools and such ideas as existed in the time of Mohammed and were spoken of in the Koran were sanctioned, all later developments being held to be the product of heathenism. Even things that had been a part of the life of former generations were at best only tolerated. An old style of gun could be used, but not a *new* one. Galleys might be used as warships, but anything of more recent date was tabooed. Nor could there be any discussion of such priestly decisions; the "door of controversy" was declared to be closed.

Uncompromising as to everything else, the ulema had little to say against any form of debauch. Indeed, many of them were themselves steeped in it, and they made no attempt to interfere with the private life of the Sultan. The selling of fetwas* also became very common.

*A "fetwa" is a religious decision delivered by an authorized religious dig-

The Dynasty.—The Empire, in its days of power, had largely maintained its strength by holding to the principle of selection. Its rulers were given their places because of their merit, fitness, training, and resourcefulness. In the era of decline, only the artful, the corrupt, and the debauched had any chance of holding their positions. There were instances where at a stroke a dancer or a gypsy was made admiral of the fleet, or general of the janissaries. As a rule positions of state were sold by those most influential to the highest bidder, and sold on the explicit understanding that the buyer would use every arbitrary means in the work of extortion, and duly share his gains with his protector in Constantinople. As every new sale of such offices promised new profits, officeholders were often changed so that each new incumbent could enter upon the work, and suck the peoples' savings dry once more. Those in power in Constantinople also derived great incomes from the presents and bribes of foreign governments. . . .

But they had also every reason for spending every ducat they got, for any right of possession of wealth of that sort was limited to the life of the possessor. Death might come at any moment, in case some rival rose to power; and on the owner's death everything was seized. As one way to prevent this, it became a matter of custom to invest one's possessions, during one's own lifetime, in pious foundations, such as mosques, religious seminaries, schools, fountains, soup kitchens, and the like. The heirs of the givers could be made perpetual guardians of such foundations, and in that way be certain of at least a small income. It was also wise not to attract attention to one's wealth by any external display. The houses of the wealthy were very simple so far as everything outside was concerned, but anything but that, within. And it was common for wealthy officials to add "the poor" to their names in the hope in that way to deceive their successors.

---

nitary to decide questions as to whether some given act is or is not in accordance with religious traditions, and, in connection therewith, what course —religious, political, or individual—should be followed.

What had been borne by those who could bear it was now shifted to the backs of the peasantry. In addition to extortions that had no pretense of legality, taxes were collected two or three times a year. The whole system was a burden so unbearable, in fact, that in wholesale migrations the peasants fled from it. Great areas could no longer be farmed. A country that had once exported grain at wholesale was now so reduced that famines became the regular thing. And many of the starving lived on animals that had died, and on wild roots and berries. It was a common thing for wolves to enter even the large towns.

The economic ruin of the Ottoman Empire cannot be ascribed simply to the change in the trade routes. That may have had its influence, but it was by no means the main thing, for long after the decline had begun, the Empire still controlled the resources of Syria and Egypt, the trade route to Persia, and also took an active part in the trade of the Mediterranean. The ruin of agricultural production and manufacturing by misgovernment and depopulation must be held to be the chief factors.

The decrease in population, an alarming decrease, was a phase of the process of breakdown which was not easy to remedy. Even successful war had demanded a toll of the best blood; and when the Empire no longer waged successful war, such human resources as Christian children, prisoners, slaves, and the inhabitants of conquered provinces were at an end. The price in blood had to be paid by the Turkish population of the home country. And as all army organization had become very bad, the army equipment worse than that of Turkey's old-time enemies, losses were far higher, proportionately, than before.

Furthermore, internal struggles were now habitual. Misgovernment was not accepted with resignation and the spirit of fatalism by the suffering people. There were ceaseless revolts. Sometimes they took the form of open rebellion, sometimes of new religious movements. In all cases merciless repressive measures followed. A hundred thousand peasants perished during the so-called "Djelali" rising. The casualties in other great rebellions were not less than 30,000. Every period of extreme anarchy was ended by some government terrorist who established order at a huge price in human life. In 1656, the Grand Vizier, Keuprulu Mehmed Pasha, sentenced 36,000 to death; and the chief executioner accounted for 4,000 with his own hand.

It became more and more hopeless for the common people to struggle against the existing evils. Turkish fatalism was not a matter of choice, nor a result of religious, racial, or climatic conditions. It was the only possible reaction to misgovernment, and to the overwhelming obstacles and misfortunes encountered in everyday life. If the people made head against them for a time, no one could expect a decreasing population with an ever-falling standard of living to resist and be proof against them forever. At a time when the population of Europe, once stationary, had begun to grow, the Ottoman Empire began to know a terrible decrease . . . Every new war meant not only a loss of territory, but also a new drain upon the vitality of the country. Enough that it was slowly dying. For three hundred years the great problem of who should inherit its territories was one of the constant causes of war in Europe. And, strangely enough, the Empire itself often took part in those wars as the ally of one of its would-be heirs. . . .

Index